GRADE K

School Specialty Publishing

Copyright © 2007 School Specialty Publishing. Published by American Education Publishing™, an imprint of School Specialty Publishing, a member of the School Specialty Family.

Send all inquiries to:
School Specialty Publishing
8720 Orion Place
Columbus, OH 43240-2111

ISBN 0-7696-7430-5

2 3 4 5 6 7 8 9 10 POH 12 11 10 09 08 07

AMERICAN
EDUCATION
PUBLISHING™
Columbus, Ohio

Table of Contents

Unit 1 5
Week 01 6
Week 02 14
Week 03 22
Review 29

Unit 2 30
Week 04 31
Week 05 39
Week 06 47
Review 54

Unit 3 55
Week 07 56
Week 08 64
Week 09 72
Review 79

Unit 4 80
Week 10 81
Week 11 89
Week 12 97
Review 104

Unit 5 105
Week 13 106
Week 14 114
Week 15 122
Review 129

Unit 6 130
Week 16 131
Week 17 139
Week 18 147
Review 154

Unit 7 155
Week 19 156
Week 20 164
Week 21 172
Review 179

Unit 8 180
Week 22 181
Week 23 189
Week 24 197
Review 204

Unit 9 205
Week 25 206
Week 26 214
Week 27 222
Review 229

Unit 10 230
Week 28 231
Week 29 239
Week 30 247
Review 254

Unit 11 255
Week 31 256
Week 32 264
Week 33 272
Review 279

Unit 12 280
Week 34 281
Week 35 289
Week 36 297
Review 304

Answer Key 305

About The Book

Connect With Words is designed to help students increase their vocabulary skills with cross-curricular, grade-appropriate words and activities.

Activity Pages

Connect With Words is divided into 36 weeks, which is the average length of the school year. Each book is broken down into three-week units with a review lesson at the conclusion of each unit. The activity pages in the book focus on important words from different subject areas.

Keywords

A keyword is listed at the bottom of each activity page. This keyword is the link that connects students to the online activities via the CD, providing extra practice.

How to Use the CD

After inserting the CD into your computer, first follow the directions to register for the online activities database. Your registration is free and good for one year. After you have registered, click on the unit that your student is currently working on. Then, click on the appropriate keyword. This will take you to an online database of activities related to that keyword. You may choose to download up to 200 activities, which you may then print. Also included on the CD is a printable progress chart so your student can keep track of his or her progress through the workbook.

For further explanation of the online database, CD, or for technical help, refer to the help me file located on the CD.

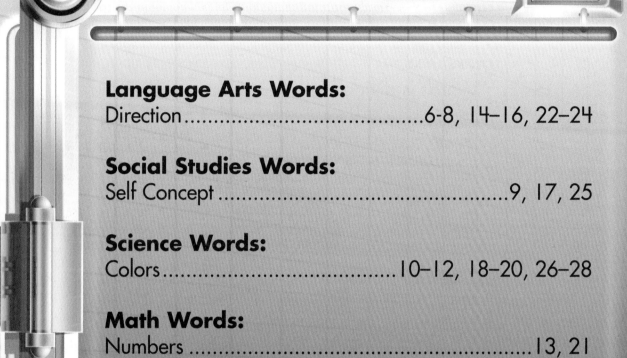

UNIT 1

Language Arts Words:
Direction...6-8, 14–16, 22–24

Social Studies Words:
Self Concept 9, 17, 25

Science Words:
Colors.......................................10–12, 18–20, 26–28

Math Words:
Numbers 13, 21

Unit 1 Review 29

Name:_____

Direction Words

Directions: The word **left** tells a direction. Look at the picture. Trace the word.

Name:_____

Direction Words

Directions: The word **right** tells a direction. Look at the picture. Trace the word.

 Directions

7

Name:_____

Direction Words

Directions: The words **left** and **right** tell direction. Color the pictures on the left blue. Color the pictures on the right red. Then, write the correct direction word under each picture.

- -

- -

Directions   8

Name:_____

Words About Me

Directions: Write your name. Then, draw a picture of yourself doing something you like.

Name:_____

Color Words

Directions: Color the word at the top of the page red. Then, color the pictures red.

10

Name:_____

Color Words

Directions: Color the word at the top of the page orange. Then, color the pictures orange.

Name:_____

Color Words

Directions: Color the word at the top of the page yellow. Then, color the pictures yellow.

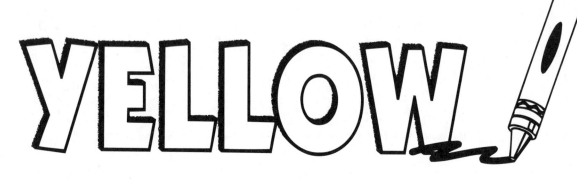

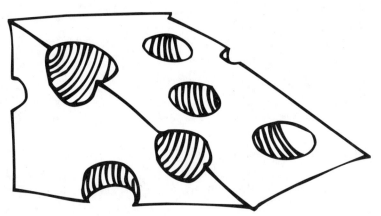

UNIT 1

Name:_____

Number Words

Directions: Trace and write the word. Then, draw an **X** on each tank that has zero fish.

zero   zero

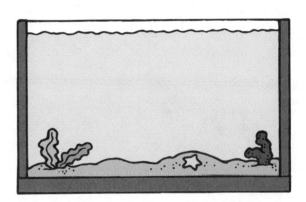

UNIT 1

Name:_____

Direction Words

Directions: Trace the lines from left to right to help each mother find her baby.

left   right

left   right

left   right

Name:_____

Direction Words

Directions: Draw a line from the picture on the left to the picture on the right in each row.

UNIT 1

Name:_____

Direction Words

Directions: The word **top** tells you **where**. Look at the picture. Trace the word.

Directions

16

social studies

Name:_____

Words About Me

Directions: Write your address. Then, draw a picture of where you live.

Name:_____

Color Words

Directions: Color the word at the top of the page green. Then, color the pictures green.

Colors

18

© 2007 School Specialty Publishing

Name:_____

UNIT 1

Color Words

Directions: Color the word at the top of the page blue. Then, color the pictures blue.

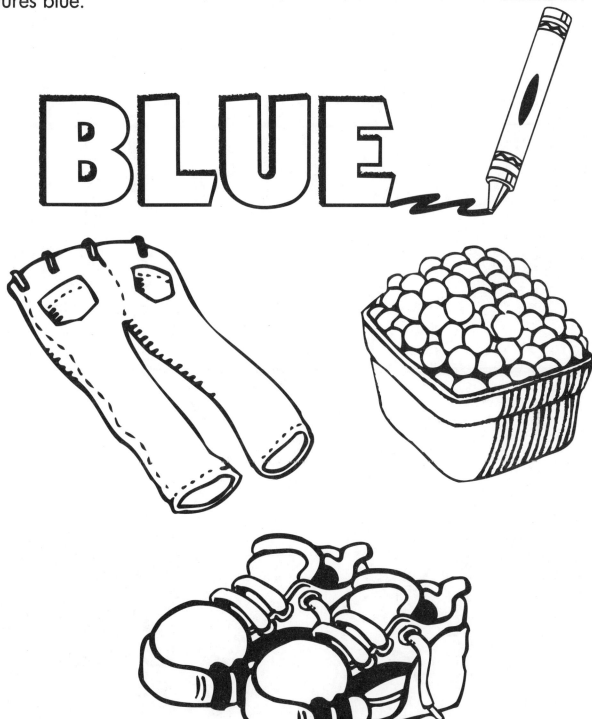

Name:_____

Color Words

Directions: Color the word at the top of the page purple. Then, color the pictures purple.

Name:_____

Number Words

Directions: Trace and write the words. Then, count the number of things in each box. Write the correct number word on the line.

one

two

- -

UNIT 1

Name: _____

Direction Words

Directions: The word **bottom** tells you **where**. Look at the picture. Trace the word.

 Directions

Name:_____

Direction Words

Directions: Trace the lines from top to bottom to help the girl paint the fence.

Name:_____

Direction Words

Directions: Trace the lines from top to bottom to help the spiders make their web.

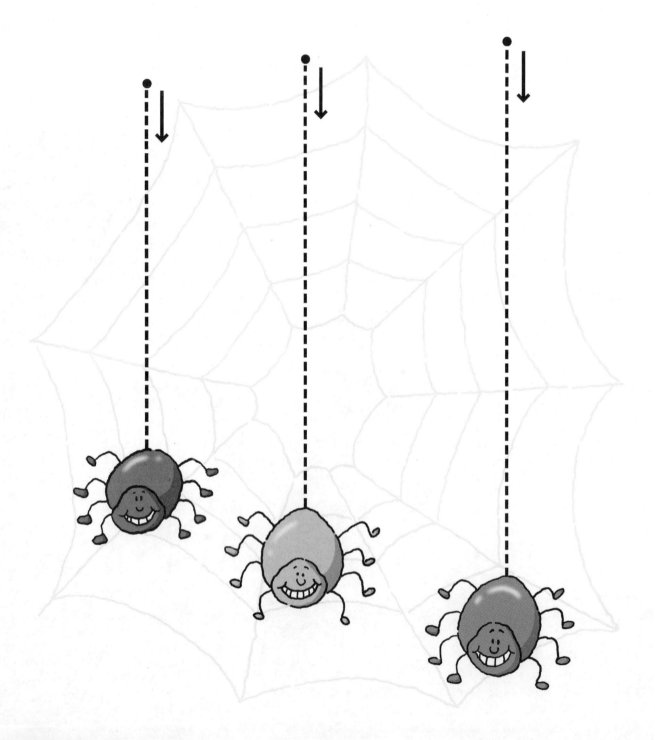

WEEK03
social studies

Name: _____

UNIT 1

Words About Me

Directions: Follow steps 1 and 2 to draw a picture of yourself.
1. Draw and color your face and hair.
2. Draw and color the clothes you wear.

Self Concept

25

© 2007 School Specialty Publishing

Name:_____

Color Words

Directions: Color the word at the top of the page black. Then, color the pictures black.

Name:_____

Color Words

Directions: Color the word at the top of the page brown. Then, color the pictures brown.

Name:_____

Color Words

Directions: Use the color words in the flowers to color the picture.

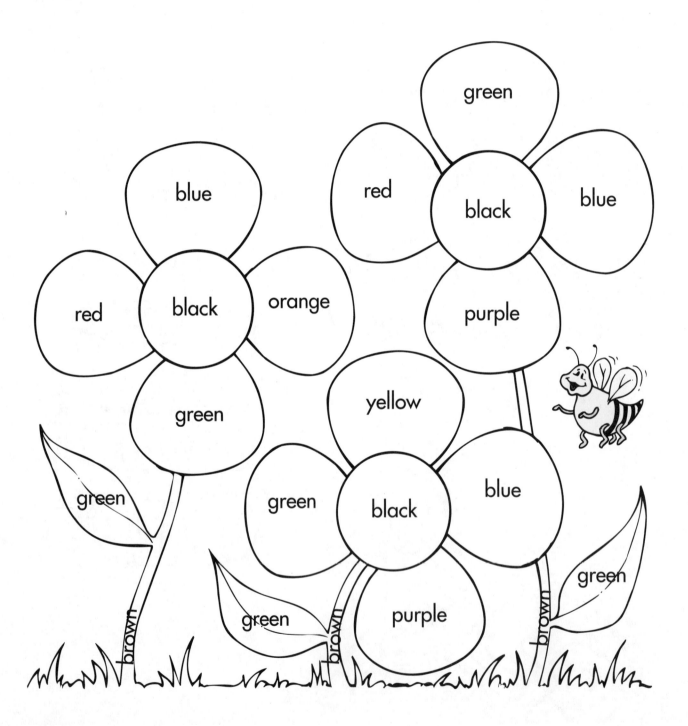

Name:_____

Unit 1 Review

Directions: Find the two things in each row that are the same color. Color them with the correct crayon. Then, circle the things on the left. Draw an X on the things on the right.

  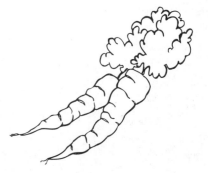

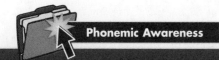

UNIT 2

Language Arts Words:
Nouns.....................................31–33, 39–41, 47–49

Social Studies Words:
Family 34, 42, 50

Science Words:
Animals 35–37, 43–45, 51–53

Math Words:
Numbers 38, 46

Unit 2 Review 54

Name:_____

Words That Name Things

Directions: Draw a line to match each word to its picture.

ball

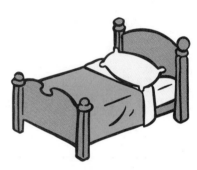

apple

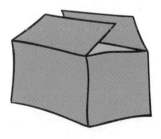

bed

box

Name:_____

UNIT 2

Words That Name Things

Directions: Draw a line to match each word to its picture.

cat

flower

car

tree

Name:_____

Words That Name Things

Directions: Draw a line to match each word to its picture.

UNIT 2

cap

log

fan

bus

net

Name:_____

Words About Family

Directions: Draw a line to match each word to its picture.

brother

sister

dad

mom

Name:_____

Animal Words

Directions: Trace each animal name. Draw a ball for each animal. Then, color the pictures.

seal

cat

dog

dolphin

Animal Words

UNIT 2

Name:_____

Directions: Name each picture. Then, write the correct letter at the beginning of each word.

_____

\- - - - - - - - - - en

_____

\- - - - - - - - - - at

_____

\- - - - - - - - - - og

_____

\- - - - - - - - - - at

Name:_____

Words That Name Things

Directions: Name each picture. Then, write the correct letter to finish the word.

b — ll   m — p   c — p

b — d   c — p   p — n

UNIT 2

Words That Name Places

Directions: Read the story. Then, circle the words that name places.

Over a hundred years ago, two men built a town. They couldn't decide what to name it. One man wanted to call it Boston. The other wanted to name it Portland. They tossed a coin and one yelled, "Heads for Boston!" The other yelled, "Tails for Portland!" Tails must have won because that town is now called Portland, Oregon.

Name:_____

Words That Name Places

Directions: Trace and write the words that name places.

farm

school

zoo

Name:_____

Words About Family

Directions: Families are made up of many different people. Look at each picture. Then, trace each word.

UNIT 2

  grandmother

 grandfather

 aunt

  uncle

  cousins

Name:_____

Animal Words

Directions: Color and cut out the pictures. Put the pictures in a pile. Then, choose a card. Describe the animal to a friend.

UNIT 2

dog

cat

fish

bug

bird

rabbit

UNIT 2

Page left blank for cutting activity.

Name:_____

School Words

Directions: Look at the pictures. Then, trace and write the words.

pen

desk

Name:_____

Words About Farm Animals

Directions: Draw a line between the fences to help the lamb get back to the barn.

lamb

barn

Name:_____

Words About Farm Animals

Directions: Draw an **X** on the animal that does not belong on the farm. Then, color the animals that do belong.

UNIT 3

seal

horse

pig

duck

Name:_____

Words About Farm Animals

Directions: Draw a line to match each baby farm animal to the parent farm animal. Then, color the pictures.

kitten

chick

calf

piglet

pig

cat

hen

cow

Name: _____

Number Words

Directions: Trace and write the words. Then, count the number of things in each box. Write the correct number word on the line.

seven — — — — — — — — — — — — — — — — — —

eight — — — — — — — — — — — — — — — — — —

- - - - - - - - - - - - - - - -   - - - - - - - - - - - - - - - -

Name:_____

Words That Describe

Directions: Big and **small** are describing words. Color the big pictures yellow. Color the small pictures green.

UNIT 3

Name:_____

Words That Describe

Directions: Circle the picture that shows something small. Then, color the picture.

Directions: Circle the picture that shows something big. Then, color the picture.

UNIT 3

Name:_____

Words That Describe

Directions: Draw a line to match each word to the picture it describes.

tall

short

old

big

Name:_____

Words About Home

Directions: Follow the steps 1 through 3 to complete the picture.

1. Draw a bathtub and sink in the bathroom.
2. Draw a bed and rug in the bedroom.
3. Draw a refrigerator and toaster in the kitchen.

UNIT 3

Bedroom   Bathroom   Kitchen

Name:_____

Words About Farm Animals

Directions: Look at each picture. Then, trace the word. At the bottom, write a sentence about farm animals. Ask an adult for help.

UNIT 3

horse

cow

pig

chicken

_ _

_ _

Words About Farm Animals

Directions: Make a memory game. Cut out the cards and place them facedown. Play the game with a partner. Take turns turning over the cards to match each mother farm animal with the correct baby farm animal.

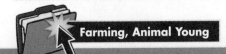

UNIT 3

Page left blank for cutting activity.

Name:_____

Number Words

Directions: Trace and write the words. Then, count the number of things in each box. Write the correct number word on the line.

nine
----

ten

-----------------------------　　　-----------------------------

Name:_____

Words That Describe

Directions: Color the small pictures green. Color the big pictures orange.

UNIT 3

Name:_____

Words That Describe

Directions: Draw a line to match each word to the picture it describes.

little

happy

sad

funny

Name:_____

Words That Describe

Directions: Color the picture in each row that both words describe.

soft and cold

tall and sad

hot and hard

Adjectives

74

© 2007 School Specialty Publishing

Name:_____

Words About Home

Directions: When someone comes home after being away, you say, "Welcome home." Trace the words. Then, draw a picture of your home.

Welcome

home

Name:_____

Words About Zoo Animals

Directions: Color the animals that live at the zoo.

UNIT 3

lion

zebra

lamb

giraffe

Zoo

76

Name:_____

Words About Zoo Animals

Directions: Help the zebra find its way to the zoo. Color the boxes from **A** to **Z**. Then, circle and name the other zoo animal in the picture.

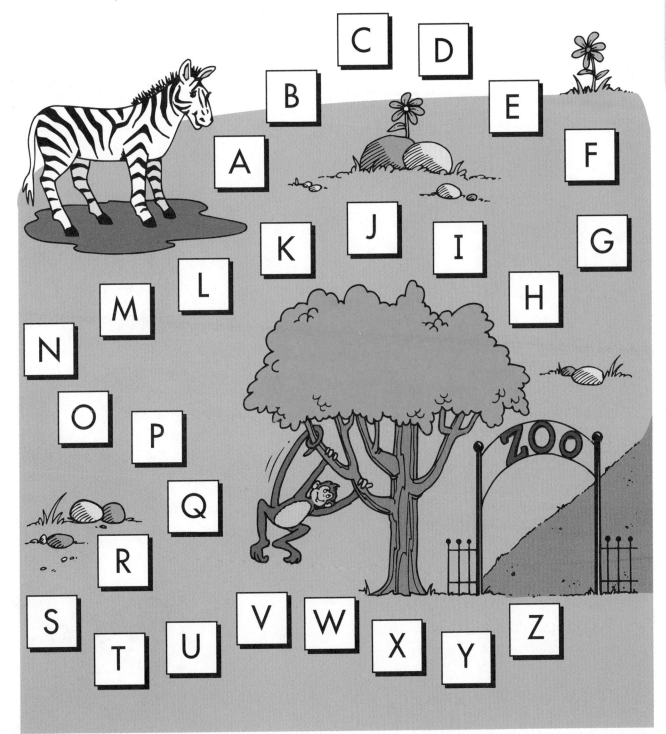

Name:_____

Words About Zoo Animals

Directions: Draw a line from each riddle to the picture that answers it.

I am black and white.

I hop and hop.

I am big. I swim.

I am big and brown.

Name:_____

Unit 3 Review

Directions: Use a word from the Word Bank to complete each sentence.

UNIT 3

Word Bank						
sink	cow	small	happy	desk	big	ten

1. I sit at a _____ when I am at school.

2. A _____ lives on a farm.

3. The number _____ comes after the number nine.

4. A piglet is _____ . Its mother is _____ .

5. I wash my hands in the _____ .

6. I am _____ when I play with my friends.

79

UNIT 4

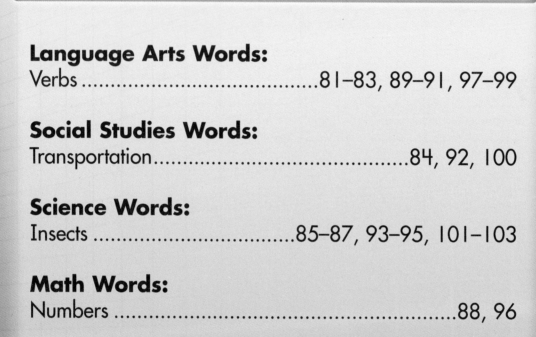

Language Arts Words:
Verbs 81–83, 89–91, 97–99

Social Studies Words:
Transportation..84, 92, 100

Science Words:
Insects 85–87, 93–95, 101–103

Math Words:
Numbers 88, 96

Unit 4 Review 104

Name:_____

Action Words

Directions: An **action word** tells what a person or thing does. Draw a line to match each action word to the person doing the action.

play

ride

sit

cook

UNIT 4

Name:_____

Action Words

Directions: Draw a line to match each action word to the person or people doing the action.

UNIT 4

walk

run

talk

eat

Name:_____

Action Words

Directions: Write the letter that completes each action word. Then, color the pictures.

Enzo can j _ _ _ _ _ _ _ mp.

Olive can cl _ _ _ _ _ _ p.

The monsters can _ _ _ _ _ _ dd.

UNIT 4

Name:_____

Transportation Words

Directions: Circle the things that have wheels.

UNIT 4

bike

skate

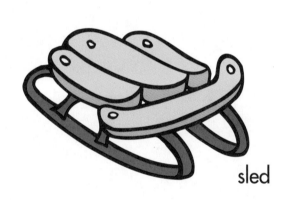

sled

wheelchair

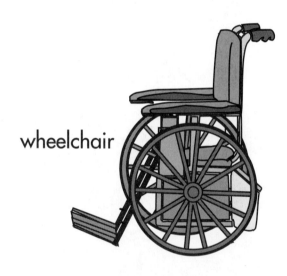

truck

wagon

Name:_____

Insect Words

Directions: Trace and write the insect word. Then, draw eight legs on each spider.

- - - spider - - - - - - - spider - - - -

- -

UNIT 4

Name:_____

Insect Words

Directions: Write each insect word on the line. Then, draw another fly and another bee.

UNIT 4

fly

bee

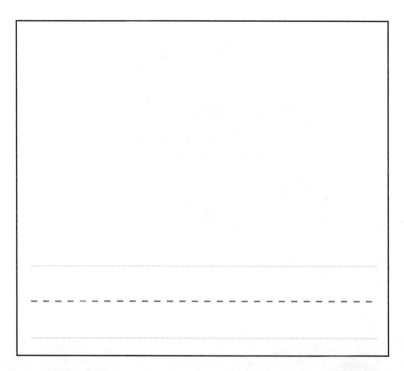

Insect Words

Directions: Read the insect words. Draw a line from each word to the part it names in the picture.

eyes

spots

wings

antennae

legs

Name:_____

Number Words

Directions: Count the beads on each string. Write the correct number word on the line.

UNIT 4

- - - - - - - - - - - - - - - - -

- - - - - - - - - - - - - - - - -

- - - - - - - - - - - - - - - - -

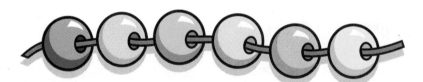

- - - - - - - - - - - - - - - - -

- - - - - - - - - - - - - - - - -

Name:_____

Action Words

Directions: Circle the action word that completes each sentence. Then, write the word on the line.

digs   **wigs**

_____

Pup _____ in the mud.

steps   **naps**

_____

Pup _____ on the rug.

hugs   **pets**

_____

Mom _____ Pup.

Name:_____

Action Words

Directions: Circle the word that completes each sentence. Then, write the word on the line.

UNIT 4

Dot will _____ the ball with her bat.

tap   tip   hop

The kids _____ on the rope.

tip   tug   sit

Can Ben _____ the pin?

tip   hit   lay

The men _____ a hole.

run   dip   dig

Pat _____ the pot in the bin.

cut   rip   put

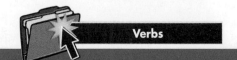

Action Words

Directions: Look at each picture. Trace the word that tells what each person does.

- - - - - - - - - - - - run - - - - - - - -

- - - - - - - hug - - - - - - - - -

- - - - - - - eat - - - - - -

- - - - - - - step - - - - -

Name:_____

Transportation Words

Directions: Read the transportation words. Then, circle the things that travel in the air.

UNIT 4

train

car

bus

airplane

ship

balloon

truck

bicycle

helicopter

Name: _____

Insect Words

Directions: Trace and write the insect word. Then, connect the dots to find out how many ladybugs there are in all. Color the ladybugs.

ladybug   ladybug

2

3

1   7

4

6

5

Name:_____

Insect Words

Directions: Draw eight spots on the ladybug. Then, point to the ladybug's antennae, head, eyes, and legs.

UNIT 4

WEEK 11
science

Name:_____

Insect Words

Directions: Read about ladybugs. Then, answer the questions.

Ladybugs are red. They have black spots. They have six legs.

1. What color are ladybugs? _____

_____

2. What color are their spots? _____

_____

3. How many legs do ladybugs have? _____

Insects

95

UNIT 4

Name:_____

Number Words

Directions: Count the rabbits in each group. Then, draw a line to match each number to the word that tells how many.

one

two

three

four

five

six

seven

eight

nine

ten

UNIT 4

Name:_____

Action Words

Directions: Cut out the action words. Then, glue each word in the correct sentence.

1. The boy ⬚ the ball.

2. The hen ⬚ in her nest.

3. I ⬚ a sandwich.

4. She can ⬚ a lot.

5. I can ⬚ you.

eat

jump

sits

kicks

run

see

UNIT 4

Page left blank for cutting activity.

Name:_____

Action Words

Directions: Color the flowers that have action words in them.

dog

play

dig

walk

bake

run

sit

man

drink

jump

Verbs

99

Name:_____

Transportation Words

Directions: Look at the pictures. Then, write the missing letter for each word.

_ b _ s _

_ v _ n

tr _ ck

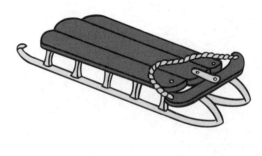

sl _ d

UNIT 4

Name:_____

Insect Words

Directions: Look at the picture. Then, read the questions. Write the correct number word.

- -

How many **butterflies** in all? _____

- -

How many **bees** in all? _____

UNIT 4

Name:_____

Insect Words

A **butterfly** is a type of insect. It has four wings.

Directions: Draw a line to connect the two matching butterflies.

Name:_____

Insect Words

Directions: Follow the steps 1 through 3 to color the butterfly. Then, trace the words.

     1. Color the spaces with 1 red.
     2. Color the spaces with 2 yellow.
     3. Color the spaces with 3 blue.

butterfly   wings

Name:_____

Unit 4 Review

Directions: Use a word from the Word Bank to complete each sentence.

Word Bank					
spider	ride	eats	talks	wagon	ladybug

My family _____ dinner together.

A _____ is an insect with wings.

We _____ the bus to school.

He pulls his toys in a _____ .

My sister _____ on the phone a lot.

A _____ has eight legs.

Language Arts Words:
Sight Words....................106–108, 114–116, 122–124

Social Studies Words:
Clothing 109, 117, 125

Science Words:
Weather......................110–112, 118–120, 126–128

Math Words:
Ordinal Numbers..113, 121

Unit 5 Review 129

Name:_____

Words You Use Often

Directions: Draw a line to match each picture to the word that names it.

men

jet

hen

web

ten

bed

UNIT 5

Name:_____

Words You Use Often

Directions: Draw a line to match each word on the left to the same word on the right.

do	have
but	the
have	and
on	do
my	a
be	was
a	but
was	my
in	be
the	on
and	in

UNIT 5

Sight Words   **107**   © 2007 School Specialty Publishing

Name:_____

Words You Use Often

Directions: Read the words. Circle the word that is the same as the first word in the row.

UNIT 5

the	the he
and	at and
in	tin in
am	am jam

Name:_____

Clothing Words

Directions: Color the pictures that are clothes.

shirt

coat

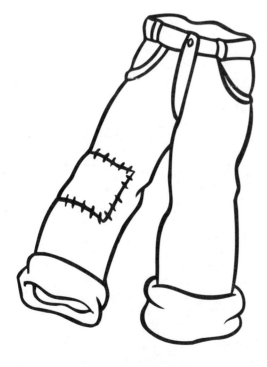

pants

car

Name:_____

Weather Words

Directions: Trace the word under each picture. Then, color the pictures.

sun

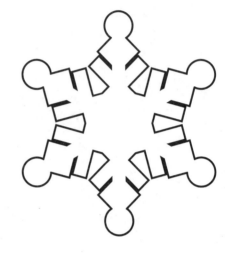

snow

cloud

rain

© 2007 School Specialty Publishing

Name:_____

Weather Words

Directions: Cut out the cards. Match the things that go with sunny, rainy, and snowy weather.

sunny

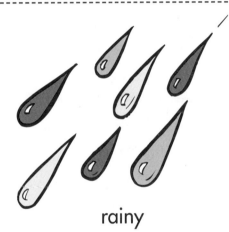

rainy

snowy

 Weather

111

UNIT 5

Page left blank for cutting activity.

Name:_____

Ordinal Number Words

Directions: Look at the train of animals. Then, write the word on the line that tells each animal's place in line.

first second third fourth fifth sixth seventh eighth ninth tenth

Ordinal Numbers

113

Name:_____

Words You Use Often

Directions: Read each word. Then, write it on the line.

look

do

the

of

to

but

had

I

my

look

he

on

all

Name: _____

Words You Use Often

Directions: Circle the two words in each row that are the same. The first one is done for you.

 to

  in

at at

is

Name: _____

Words You Use Often

Directions: Look at each picture. Write the words from the Word Bank that finish each sentence. The first one is done for you.

Word Bank		
fat	red	big
bed	pig	cat

The bed is red.

The _____ is _____ .

The _____ is _____ .

UNIT 5

Name:_____

Clothing Words

Directions: Look at the pictures of clothes. Trace the words. Then, read them aloud.

pants

sock

vest

UNIT 5

Name:_____

Weather Words

Directions: It is raining. This boy wants to play outside. Circle the things he needs to use to stay dry.

earmuffs

raincoat

boots

umbrella

backpack

skis

hat

Name:_____

Weather Words

Directions: You wear different things depending on the weather. Draw a picture to show what else you would wear for each type of weather.

Things for Warm Weather

Things for Cold Weather

Things for Rainy Weather

UNIT 5

Name:_____

Weather Words

Directions: Read this story with an adult.

The itsy bitsy went the  .

 came the and washed the out.

Out came the and dried  all the .

And the itsy bitsy went  the again.

spider	up	water	spout
down	rain	sun	

UNIT 5

Name:_____

Ordinal Number Words

Directions: Follow steps 1 through 5 to complete the activity.
1. **Draw** a box around the **second** person in line.
2. **Draw** a line above the **fourth** person in line.
3. **Draw** an **X** on the **first** person in line.
4. **Draw** a line under the **fifth** person in line.
5. **Circle** the **third** person in line.

Name:_____

Words You Use Often

Directions: Write the word on the line that answers each riddle. Use the words at the bottom of the page.

UNIT 5

This can spin fast.

This can ring and ring.

This is a soft pet.

This holds food.

This is very hot.

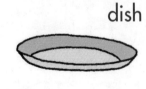

bell

cat

dish

sun

top

Name:_____

Words You Use Often

Directions: Cut out the cards. Read the words. Then, match each word to its picture.

hat	van	bat	ham
bag	man	map	fan

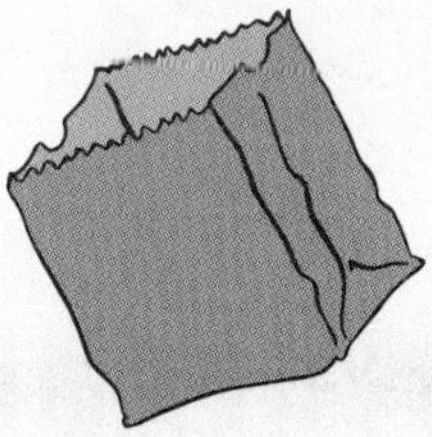

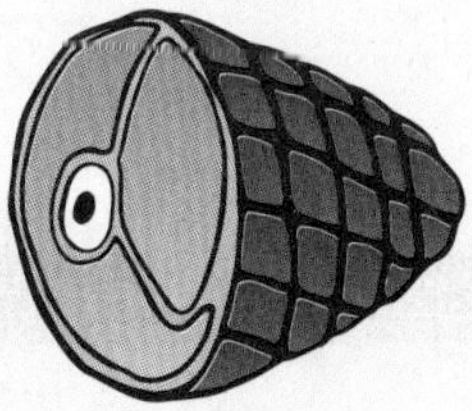

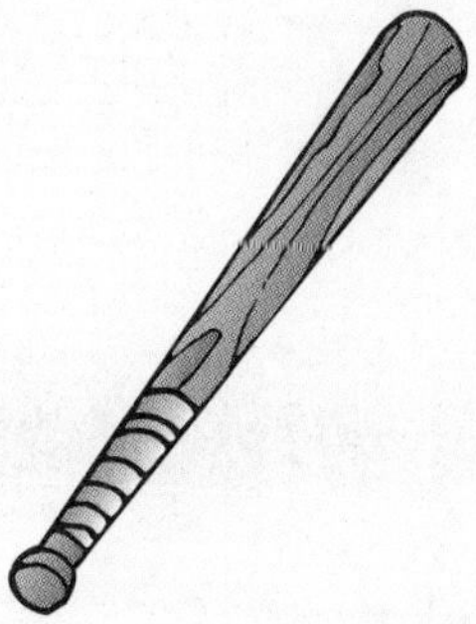

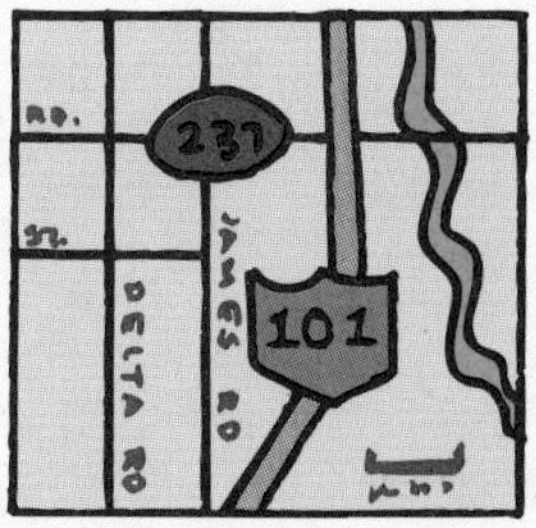

UNIT 5

Page left blank for cutting activity.

Name:_____

Clothing Words

Directions: Look at all these hats! Trace and write the word. Then, draw a picture of a funny hat.

hat

Name:_____

Weather Words

Directions: Connect the dots from 1 to 10. Answer the question at the bottom of the page. Then, color the picture.

What is fun to play with on a windy day? _____

Name:_____

Weather Words

Directions: Circle the word that completes each sentence. Then, write the word on the line.

1. Today is a _____ day.   **hit**   **hot**

2. I hope it won't _____ .   **rain**   **pain**

3. It will get _____ later.   **cool**   **pool**

Name:_____

Weather Words

Directions: Use the words in the Word Bank to complete the story.

Word Bank			
snow	ice	wind	cold

Maria dresses warmly to go outside.

_____ _____

_____ is falling. _____ is

_____

hanging from the roof. The _____ blows Maria's scarf

_____

around. It is very _____ outside! Here come Maria's

friends for a snowball fight!

Name:_____

Unit 5 Review

Directions: Use the Word Bank to find the word that is being described in each sentence. Write the word on the line.

Word Bank					
cat	coat	bed	sun	fifth	man

1. This shines on a hot, summer day.

- -

2. This is a popular pet.

- -

3. This number comes after fourth.

- -

4. This is a grown-up boy.

- -

5. You wear this when it is cold outside.

- -

6. You sleep in this.

UNIT 5

UNIT 6

Language Arts Words:
Prepositions.....................131–133, 139–141, 147–149

Social Studies Words:
Holidays...134, 142, 150

Science Words:
Seasons 135–137, 143–145, 151–153

Math Words:
Shapes 138, 146

Unit 6 Review 154

Name: _____

Position Words

Directions: On, **beside**, **under**, and **in** are position words. Follow steps 1 through 4 to complete the picture.

1. Draw a ladybug **on** the rock.

2. Draw a tree **beside** the rock.

3. Draw a butterfly **under** the birdbath.

4. Draw a bird **in** the birdbath.

Position Words

Directions: Between is a position word. Trace and color the cat that is between the other cats.

Directions: Color the mouse that is between the other mice.

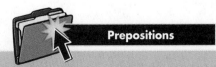

Name:_____

Position Words

Directions: Over is a position word. Color the skunk that hit the ball over the grass.

UNIT 6

Holiday Words

Valentine's Day is a holiday that happens every year on February 14. On this day, you think about the people you love, and you send them valentines.

Directions: Trace the words. Then, write the words on the heart. Color the heart.

I love you.

Name:_____

Winter Words

Directions: Color the pictures that show winter words.

snowman

watermelon

mitten

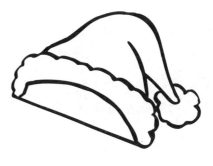

hat

135

UNIT 6

Name:_____

Winter Words

Directions: Circle the pictures that show winter words.

shell

boat

fish

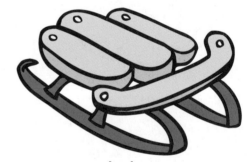

sled

snowman

pail

Name: _____

Spring Words

Directions: Sometimes, it rains a lot in the spring. The rain helps flowers grow. Color the flowers. Then, trace and write the word.

spring

Name:_____

Shape Words

A **circle** is a round shape.

Directions: Trace the circles. Then, color the pictures.

Name:_____

Position Words

Directions: Color and cut out the pictures at the bottom of the page. Then, glue them in the correct places.

under

on

between

in

UNIT 6

UNIT 6

Page left blank for cutting activity.

Name:_____

Position Words

Directions: Above and **below** are position words. Color the pictures above the clouds yellow. Then, color the pictures below the clouds blue.

UNIT 6

Holiday Words

Thanksgiving is a holiday in November. On this day, you think about the things you are thankful for.

Directions: Trace the words. Color the picture. Then, use the words to tell about Thanksgiving.

thanks

family

turkey

UNIT 6

Name:_____

Summer Words

Directions: Summer at the beach is fun! Follow steps 1 through 5 to complete the picture.

1. Color the umbrella yellow and purple.
2. Color the big beach ball red and blue.
3. Circle the boat.
4. Draw two blue fish in the water.
5. Draw a yellow sun in the sky.

Name:_____

Summer Words

Directions: Trace and write the summer words. Then, use the words to talk about the picture.

pool

fun

friends

water

Name:_____

Summer Words

Directions: Look at the words and pictures. Then, draw two more pictures of summer things.

sun		sandals	
flowers		fruit tree	
garden		car with open window	
blue sky		pool	
sprinkler			
shorts			

UNIT 6

Name:_____

Shape Words

A **square** is a shape with four equal sides.

Directions: Trace the word. Then, circle the square in each row.

 square

UNIT 6

Position Words

Directions: Above and **below** are position words. Read the sentences. Draw a line to match each animal to its cage.

1. The lion goes below the monkey.
2. The tiger goes above the monkey.
3. The monkey goes above the lion and below the tiger.

Name:_____

lion

tiger

monkey

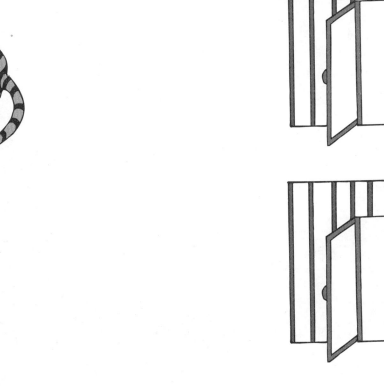

Prepositions

UNIT 6

Name: _____

Position Words

Directions: Above is a position word. Look at the picture. The sun is above the bird. Circle the other things above the bird.

UNIT 6

language arts

Name:_____

Position Words

Directions: Between is a position word. Find the shape in each row that is between the other shapes. Color it.

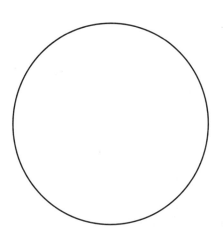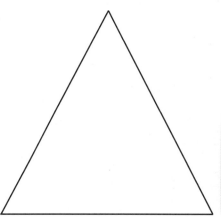

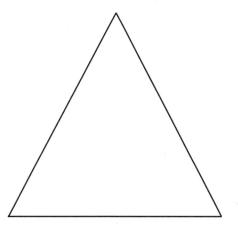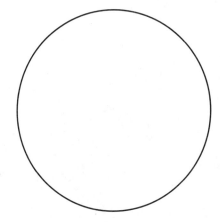

Prepositions

© 2007 School Specialty Publishing

Name:_____

Holiday Words

Americans celebrate the **Fourth of July** every year. It is the birthday of the United States. Americans celebrate with parades and fireworks.

Directions: Trace the words. Then, use them to tell about the Fourth of July.

fireworks

parade

Name:_____

Fall Words

Directions: It is fun to rake the fall leaves! Color the leaves with **L** orange. Color the leaves with **I** red.

Name:_____

Words About the Seasons

Directions: In the winter, it is cold outside. The daytime is short. Sometimes it snows. Color the children who are dressed for winter.

Directions: In the summer, it is warm outside. The daytime is long. The sun shines a lot. Color the children who are dressed for summer.

UNIT 6

Name:_____

Words About the Seasons

Directions: Follow steps 1 through 4 to complete the pictures. Trace the words. Then, color the pictures.

1. **Draw** a rake in the picture of **fall**.
2. **Draw** a sled in the picture of **winter**.
3. **Draw** a butterfly in the picture of **spring**.
4. **Draw** a swimming pool in the picture of **summer**.

fall

winter

spring

summer

UNIT 6

Name:_____

Unit 6 Review

Directions: Circle the position word in each sentence.

1. The dog hides under the table.

2. I sit between my two friends in class.

3. The ladybug sits on a rock.

4. The plane flies over the house.

Directions: Circle the season word described in each sentence.

The air is cool. Leaves are falling from the trees. We help rake them up.

winter   spring   summer   fall

The sun is bright and hot. We swim in the pool to cool off.

winter   spring   summer   fall

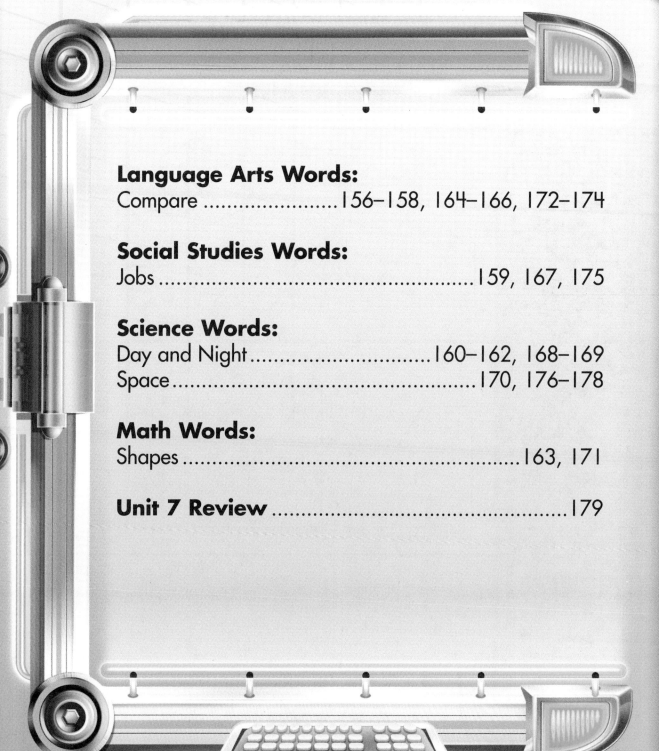

Language Arts Words:
Compare 156–158, 164–166, 172–174

Social Studies Words:
Jobs 159, 167, 175

Science Words:
Day and Night 160–162, 168–169
Space 170, 176–178

Math Words:
Shapes 163, 171

Unit 7 Review 179

Name:_____

Words That Compare

Directions: Same and **different** are words that compare. Color the shape in each row that looks the same as the first shape.

Name:_____

Words That Compare

Directions: Taller and **shorter** are words that compare two things. Circle the thing in each box that is taller than the other.

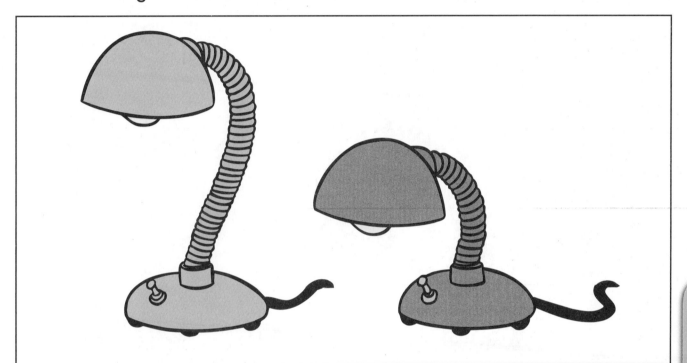

UNIT 7

Name:_____

Words That Compare

Directions: Longest is a word that compares three or more things.
Circle the longest thing in each row. The first one is done for you.

UNIT 7

Name:_____

Job Words

Directions: Bob is a **baker**. A baker makes bread, cakes, and muffins. Circle the things Bob needs to do his job. At the bottom of the page, draw some treats from his bakery. Write the names of these treats.

Model Airplane

SALT

UNIT 7

Name:_____

Time of Day Words

Directions: Night is the time when it is dark outside. Circle the things you usually do at night.

_____

Directions: Day is the time when it is light outside. Draw a picture of something you do only in the day.

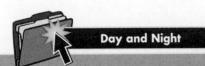

Name:_____

Time of Day Words

Directions: Draw a picture of something in the night sky.

day | night

Directions: Draw a picture of something you do at night.

UNIT 7

Name:_____

Time of Day Words

Directions: Look at the pictures. Then, trace the words. Read them aloud.

Good morning

Good night

UNIT 7

Name:_____

Shape Words

A **rectangle** is a shape with two long sides and two short sides.

Directions: Trace the word. Then, color each rectangle the correct color.

rectangle

green

yellow

blue

red

orange

purple

UNIT 7

Name:_____

Words That Compare

Directions: Shortest is a word that compares three or more things. Circle the shortest thing in each row. The first one is done for you.

UNIT 7

Name:_____

Words That Compare

Directions: Color the longest thing in each row. Then, draw an **X** on the shortest thing in each row.

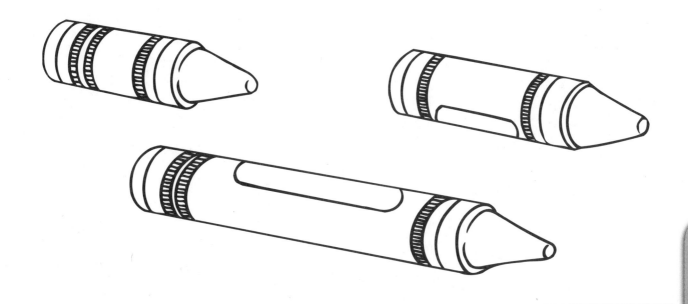

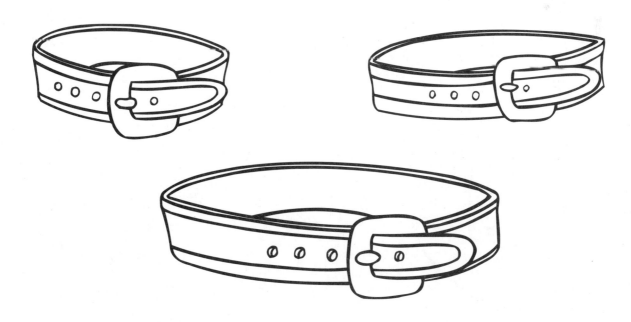

UNIT 7

Name:_____

Words That Compare

Directions: Biggest and **smallest** are words that compare three or more things. Color the biggest thing in each row. Then, circle the smallest thing in each row.

UNIT 7

Name:_____

Job Words

Directions: Draw a line to match each person with the name of his or her job.

firefighter   carpenter   baker   baseball player

UNIT 7

Name:_____

Time of Day Words

Directions: Color the things you see in the night sky.

moon

star

sun

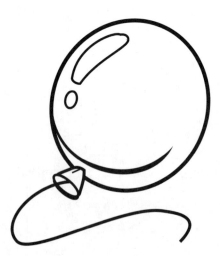

balloon

UNIT 7

Name:_____

Time of Day Words

Directions: Trace and write the word.

star

Directions: Circle the word **star** each time you read it in the poem.

Twinkle, twinkle little star.
How I wonder what you are.
Up above the world so high,
Like a diamond in the sky.
Twinkle, twinkle little star.
How I wonder what you are.

UNIT 7

Name:_____

Space Words

Directions: Color each picture with the word **moon** or **star** in it.

UNIT 7

Name:_____

Shape Words

A **triangle** is a shape with three sides.

Directions: Trace the word. Then, color each triangle the correct color.

triangle

UNIT 7

Name:_____

Words That Compare

Directions: Shortest is a word that compares three or more things. Color the shortest thing in each row. The first one is done for you.

UNIT 7

Name:_____

Words That Compare

Directions: Smallest and **biggest** are words that compare three or more things. Cut out the pictures. Then, put the animals in order from smallest to biggest.

UNIT 7

Page left blank for cutting activity.

Name:_____

Job Words

A **barber** cuts and styles hair. He works in a **barber shop**.

Directions: Circle the tools a barber might need. At the bottom of the page, draw something else he might need to do his job.

UNIT 7

Name:_____

Space Words

Word Bank

| comet | moon | rocket | Mars | star | planet |

Directions: Use the words in the Word Bank to find the rockets that contain space words. Then, color the rockets.

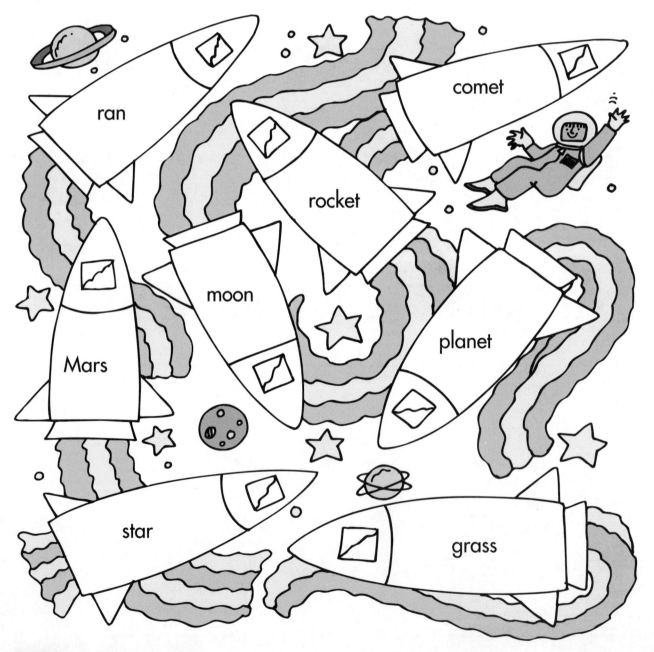

UNIT 7

Name:_____

Space Words

Directions: Color the pictures of things you might find in space.

astronaut

moon

ant

rocket

UNIT 7

Name:_____

Space Words

Directions: Trace and write the space words.

star

rocket

planet

moon

UNIT 7

Name:_____

Unit 7 Review

Directions: Draw a line to match each word to its description.

day   something you see in the night sky

smallest   someone who makes bread

baker   opposite of biggest

star   when it is light outside

Directions: Draw each shape.

1. triangle   2. rectangle

UNIT 7

179   © 2007 School Specialty Publishing

Language Arts Words:
Synonyms 181–183, 189–191, 197–199

Social Studies Words:
Feelings.. 184, 192, 200

Science Words:
Plants........................ 185–187, 193–195, 201–203

Math Words:
Shapes 188, 196

Unit 8 Review 204

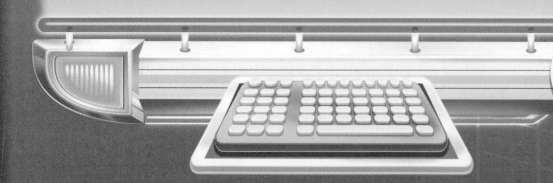

Name:_____

Words That Mean the Same Thing

Directions: Look at the pictures and the words that name them. Then, circle the word in each row that means the same thing as the first word.

icy   cold   hot

gloomy   red   dark

happy   cheerful   frown

jump   walk   leap

UNIT 8

Name:_____

Words That Mean the Same Thing

Directions: Read the sentences. Then, use the Word Bank to find the word that means the same thing as the word in blue. Write the word on the line.

Word Bank			
easy	right	huge	clean

1. The dinosaur is _____ .

   big

2. She keeps her room _____ .

   tidy

3. This math problem is _____ .

   simple

4. I got the _____ answer.

   correct

Name:_____

Words That Mean the Same Thing

Directions: Read each word. Find the word on the anthill that means the same thing. Then, write the word on the line.

1. glad ----------------------------

2. little ----------------------------

3. begin ----------------------------

4. above ----------------------------

5. damp ----------------------------

6. large ----------------------------

wet

big

happy

over

small

start

UNIT 8

183

Name:_____

Words About Feelings

Directions: Read the words about feelings. Then, draw a picture of yourself when you are sad or happy.

sad

happy

UNIT 8

Name:_____

Plant Words

Directions: Read about plants. Then, answer the questions.

A plant grows from a seed.
A plant needs water and light to grow.
A plant can grow in a pot or in the ground.

1. What grows into a plant?

2. What are two things a plant needs to grow?

3. Where are two places a plant can grow?

Name:_____

Plant Words

Directions: Read about weeds. Then, answer the questions.

A **weed** is any plant that grows where people do not want it to grow. Weeds can grow fast. They make it harder for other plants to grow. The wind spreads the seeds from weeds. Birds and other animals also carry the seeds. Weeds are hard to get rid of.

1. What is a weed?

2. Do people want weeds in their gardens?

3. What are two things that spread the seeds of weeds?

UNIT 8

Name: _____

Plant Words

Directions: Use the words in the Word Bank to write the parts of the plant.

Word Bank			
roots	stem	leaf	flower

- -

- - - - - - - - - - - - - - - -   - - - - - - - - - - - - - - - -

- - - - - - - - - - - - - - - -

Name:_____

Shape Words

A **star** is a shape with five points.

Directions: Trace and write the word. Then, draw five more stars in the picture.

star

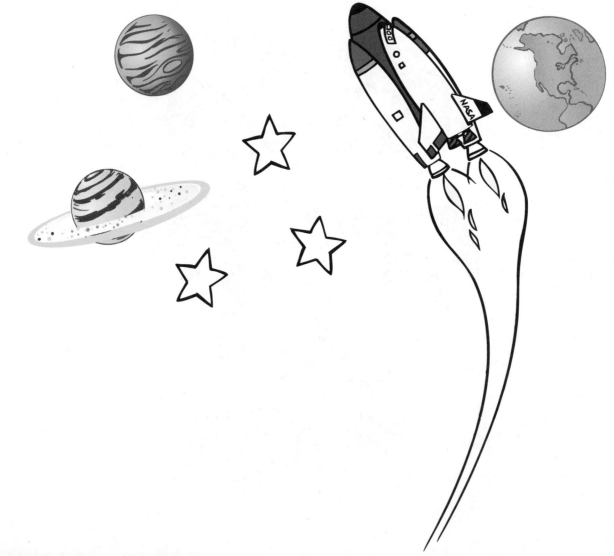

Name:_____

Words That Mean the Same Thing

Directions: Look at each picture and the word that describes it. Find a word in the Word Bank that is the same. Then, write the word on the line.

Word Bank				
afraid	tiny	loud	wet	warm

hot

_____

small

_____

damp

_____

scared

_____

noisy

_____

UNIT 8

Name:_____

Words That Mean the Same Thing

Directions: Use the Word Bank to find the word that means the same thing as the underlined word in each sentence. Then, write the word on the line.

Word Bank			
sweet	fast	friend	rock

1. Henry is my <u>pal</u>.

- -

2. The cake is <u>sugary</u>.

- -

3. I throw a <u>stone</u> in the lake.

- -

4. She is very <u>quick</u>.

UNIT 8

Name:_____

Words That Mean the Same Thing

Directions: There are many ways to tell how you feel. Look at each picture and the word that names it in the first column. Then, draw a line to match the words that are the same in the second column.

timid

scared

angry

shy

cheerful

mad

unhappy

sad

afraid

happy

Name:_____

Words About Feelings

Directions: Circle each happy face in the crowd. Then, trace the word on the balloon. Draw a happy face on the clown.

UNIT 8

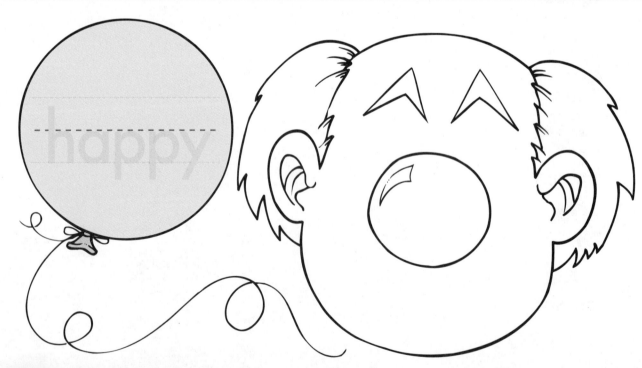

happy

Name: _____

Plant Words

Directions: Fruits and **vegetables** come from plants. Color the fruits and vegetables. Then, name them.

193

Name:_____

Plant Words

Directions: Flowers are plants with petals, stems, and leaves. Draw the missing stems. Draw leaves on the stems. Then, color the flowers.

UNIT 8

Name:_____

Plant Words

Lemons and **bananas** are fruit that grow on trees. **Corn** is a vegetable that grows up from the ground.

Directions: Draw something else that grows up from the ground. Then, color the pictures.

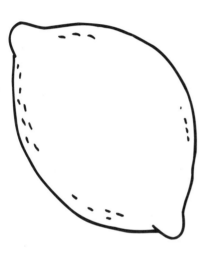

lemon

corn

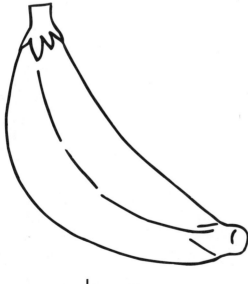

banana

© 2007 School Specialty Publishing

UNIT 8

Name:_____

Shape Words

Directions: Draw a line from each shape on the left to the shape that is the same on the right.

square

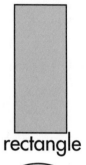

rectangle

circle

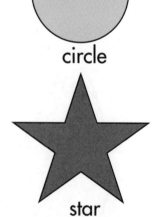

star

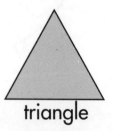

triangle

UNIT 8

Name:_____

Words That Mean the Same Thing

Directions: Use the Word Bank to find the word that means the same thing as the underlined word in each sentence. Then, write the word.

Word Bank			
hog	tiny	throw	lady

1. A kitten is a <u>small</u> cat.

2. My mom is a <u>woman</u>.

3. A <u>pig</u> lives on a farm.

4. I <u>toss</u> the ball with my dad.

197

Name:_____

Words That Mean the Same Thing

Directions: Draw a line to match each word on the left to the word on the right that means the same thing.

grin   boat

house   messy

dirty   home

good   smile

ship   nice

UNIT 8

Name:_____

Words That Mean the Same Thing

Directions: Look at each picture. Then, write two words from the Word Bank that tell about each picture. The two words should mean the same thing.

Word Bank							
rocks	start	road	begin	street	stones	sad	unhappy

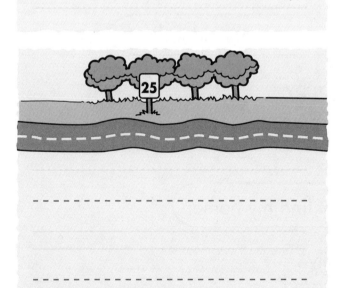

- - - - - - - - - - - - - - - - - - - -

- - - - - - - - - - - - - - - - - - - -

- - - - - - - - - - - - - - - - - - - -

- - - - - - - - - - - - - - - - - - - -

- - - - - - - - - - - - - - - - - - - -

- - - - - - - - - - - - - - - - - - - -

Synonyms

199

Name:_____

Words About Feelings

Directions: Look at each picture. Then, circle the word that tells what the animal or person is feeling.

My tummy hurts.

sick
well

My hat is blowing away.

surprised
angry

I am seven years old today.

happy
sad

I can't find my home.

silly
scared

Emotions

200

UNIT 8

Name:_____

Plant Words

Directions: Jack planted magic seeds. These seeds grew down, not up. Draw what Jack found when he followed his plant. Then, trace the words.

seed

plant

Plants

UNIT 8

Name:_____

Plant Words

Directions: First, Ben planted some seeds. Then, he watered the seeds. The sun shined on them. What happened next? Circle the correct picture. Then, trace and write the word.

flower

Name:_____

Plant Words

Directions: Gardening is fun! Color the picture. Then, circle the things that are named in the Word Bank.

Word Bank

roots

leaves

rake

tree

UNIT 8

Name:_____

Unit 8 Review

Directions: Draw lines to match the words that mean the same thing.

hot   easy

happy   small

above   warm

simple   glad

large   over

tiny   big

Directions: Use the words in the Word Bank to draw a picture of a plant. Then, label the plant parts.

UNIT 8

Word Bank
seed
pot
flower
stem
leaf
roots

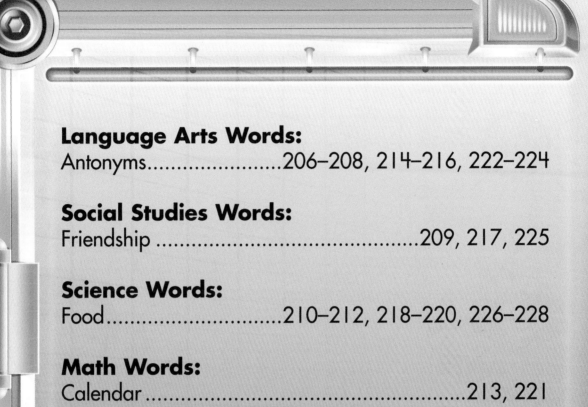

Language Arts Words:
Antonyms.......................206–208, 214–216, 222–224

Social Studies Words:
Friendship 209, 217, 225

Science Words:
Food...........................210–212, 218–220, 226–228

Math Words:
Calendar 213, 221

Unit 9 Review 229

Name:_____

Words That Are Opposites

Directions: Opposites are things that are different in every way. Draw lines to match the opposites.

day

little

front

sad

happy

night

big

back

Name:_____

Words That Are Opposites

Directions: Look at the word and picture in each row. Then, draw a picture of the opposite.

day   night

sad   happy

Name:_____

Words That Are Opposites

Directions: Look at the word and picture in each row. Then, draw a picture of the opposite.

wet   dry

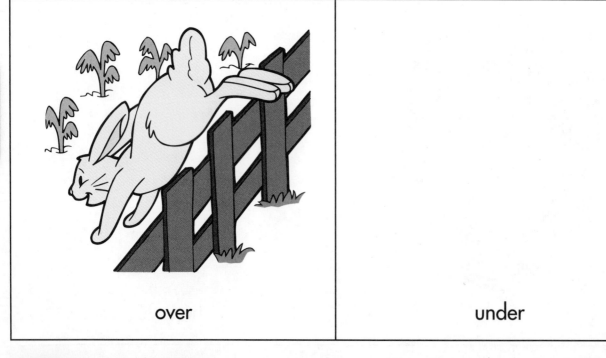

over   under

UNIT 9

Name:_____

Words About Friendship

Directions: Trace and write the words. Then, use the words to tell about the picture.

share

friends

play

UNIT 9

Name:_____

Food Words

Directions: Draw a line to match each group of food to the meal it will make. Then, say the name of each finished meal.

pancakes

milkshake

spaghetti

hamburger

sandwiches

UNIT 9

Name: _____

Food Words

Directions: This hippo loves pizza!
Pepperoni, mushrooms, and olives are
its favorite toppings. Trace the
dotted lines. Color the picture.
Then, answer the question.

- -

What do you like on your pizza?

Food

211

UNIT 9

Name:_____

Food Words

Directions: Crackers and **pretzels** are popular snack foods. Color the snack foods. Then, draw other snack foods that you like to eat.

What is your favorite snack food? _____

UNIT 9

Name:_____

Calendar Words

The days of the week are **Sunday**, **Monday**, **Tuesday**, **Wednesday**, **Thursday**, **Friday**, and **Saturday**. Saturday and Sunday make up the **weekend**.

Sunday 1	Monday 2	Tuesday 3	Wednesday 4	Thursday 5	Friday 6	Saturday 7

Directions: Look at the calendar above. Then, answer the questions.

1. Circle the first day of the week.
   Sunday   Monday   Thursday   Wednesday

2. Circle the last day of the week.
   Friday   Saturday

3. Which two days make up the weekend?

   -      - - - - - - - - - - - - - - - -

4. Write the name of your favorite day of the week.

   -

UNIT 9

Words That Are Opposites

Directions: Draw lines to match the opposites.

old

girl

boy

full

open

new

empty

closed

UNIT 9

Name:_____

Words That Are Opposites

Opposites are things that are different. **Up** and **down** are opposites. **Top** and **bottom** are opposites.

Directions: Color and cut out the children. Then, glue the girl **up** at the **top** of the slide. Glue the boy **down** at the **bottom** of the slide.

UNIT 9

UNIT 9

Page left blank for cutting activity.

Name:_____

Words About Friendship

Directions: Use the words in the Word Bank to talk about the picture.

Word Bank
birthday   party   children   sorry   happy

Name:_____

Food Words

Directions: Color the vegetables to help the rabbit find the path to the garden. Use the words in the Word Bank to point to the vegetable each word names.

Word Bank					
tomato	carrot	corn	peas	potato	lettuce

UNIT 9

Food

218

Name:_____

Food Words

Directions: Say the names of each food. Listen to the ending sound. Then, write the ending sound for each word. Color the pictures.

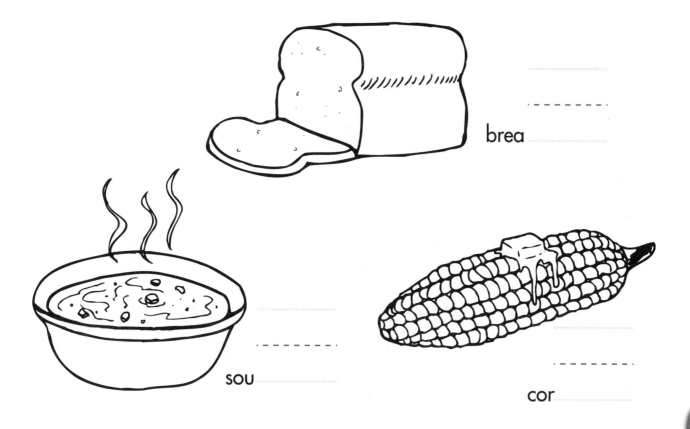

brea _ _ _ _ _ _ _

sou _ _ _ _ _ _ _

cor _ _ _ _ _ _ _

frui _ _ _ _ _ _ _

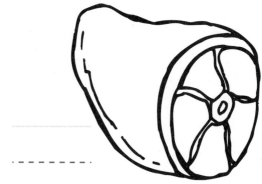

ha _ _ _ _ _ _ _

UNIT 9

Name:_____

Food Words

Directions: Follow steps 1 through 3 to color the ice-cream cone. Then, trace the words.

    1. The top scoop is chocolate.
    2. The middle scoop is vanilla.
    3. The bottom scoop is strawberry.

ice cream

UNIT 9

Name:_____

Calendar Words

Directions: Use the calendar to complete each sentence. Circle the correct answer. Then, color your birthday month.

January	February	March	April
1	BE MINE 2	3	4
May	June	July	August
5	6	7	8
September	October	November	December
9	10	11	12

1. January is the _____ month of the year.
   ninth   twelfth   first   second

2. December comes after_____ .
   October   February   November   May

3. The month before September is _____ .
   January   August   November   June

4. There are _____ months in every year.
   four   twelve   sixteen   eleven

5. The third month of the year is _____ .
   February   March   May   April

UNIT 9

Words That Are Opposites

Directions: Draw lines to match the opposites.

left

out

above

right

in

below

UNIT 9

Name:_____

Words That Are Opposites

Directions: Color and cut out the birds. Glue one bird **over** the rainbow. Glue the other bird **under** the rainbow. Then, color the rainbow.

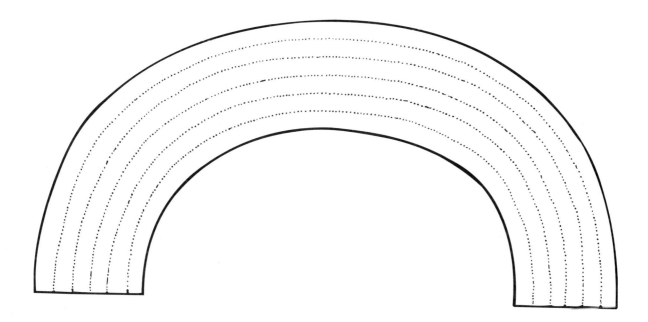

Page left blank for cutting activity.

Name:_____

Words About Friendship

Directions: These two girls are playing hopscotch. Use the words in the Word Bank to talk about the picture.

Word Bank				
girls	play	wait	fun	take turns

UNIT 9

Name:_____

Food Words

Directions: A sandwich and grapes are good for lunch. Color the pictures. Then, answer the questions.

sandwich

- -

What is your favorite sandwich?_____

grapes

- -

What color are your favorite grapes?_____

UNIT 9

Name:_____

Food Words

Directions: Cut out the cards. Put the picture cards in one pile. Put the word cards in another pile. Choose a card from each pile. If the picture matches the word, keep the cards. If not, put them back and try again.

cookie

apple

sandwich

UNIT 9

Page left blank for cutting activity.

UNIT 9

Name:_____

Unit 9 Review

Directions: Trace the word in each row. Then, draw a picture to show its opposite.

day

over

sad

small

girl

Directions: Think about your favorite month of the year. Tell someone why you like it.

Language Arts Words:
Sequence 231–233, 239–241, 247–249

Social Studies Words:
Communities...234, 242, 250

Science Words:
The Human Body............235–237, 243–245, 251–253

Math Words:
Fractions...238, 246

Unit 10 Review...254

Name:_____

Sequence Words

Directions: First is a sequence word. It tells when something happens. Color the pictures. Then, circle the picture in each row that shows what happened first.

  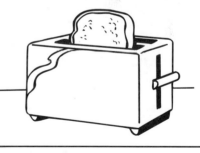

Name:_____

Sequence Words

Directions: Next is a sequence word. It tells when something happens. Color the pictures in each row that shows what comes after the first picture. Then, circle the picture.

UNIT 10

Name: _____

Sequence Words

Directions: Last is a sequence word. It tells when something happens. Color the pictures. Then, circle the picture in each row that shows what happened last.

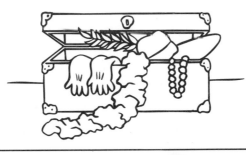

UNIT 10

Name:_____

Words About Living in a City

Directions: Look at the picture. Use the words in the Word Bank to tell what you think it would be like to live in the city. Then, trace and write the word.

Word Bank			
tall	buildings	apartments	crowds
stores	noisy	people	park

city

Name:_____

Words About the Human Body

Directions: Trace and write the word. Then, answer the question.

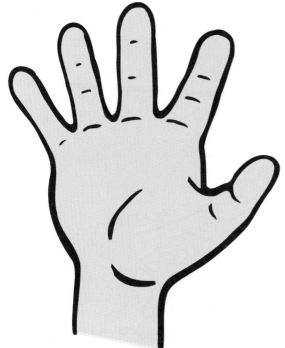

hands

- -

- -

UNIT 10

- -

How many fingers are there in all? _____

WEEK 28
science

Name:_____

Words About the Human Body

Directions: Trace and write the word. Then, answer the question.

feet

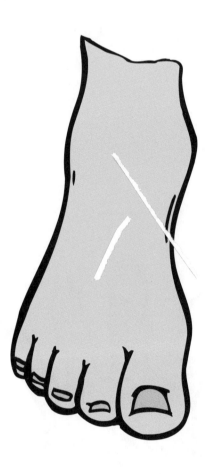

How many toes are there in all?_____

Human Body

236

© 2007 School Specialty Publishing

UNIT 10

Name:_____

Words About the Human Body

Directions: Trace and write the words. Then, color the picture.

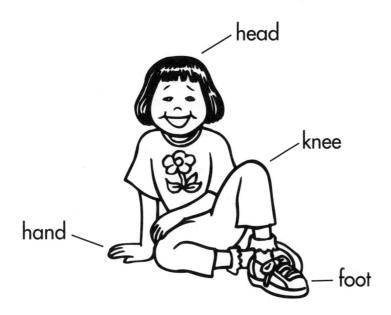

head

knee

hand

foot

head

hand

knee

foot

UNIT 10

Human Body

237

Name:_____

Words About Fractions

Directions: When a shape is divided into two equal parts, each part is called a **half**. Draw the other half of each kite to match. Then, color the kites.

UNIT 10

Name: _____

Sequence Words

Directions: Last is a sequence word. It tells when something happens. Color the pictures. Then, circle the picture in each row that shows what happened last.

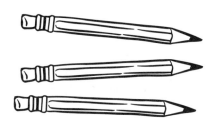 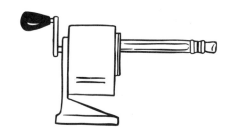 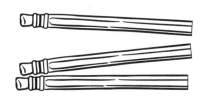

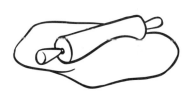  

 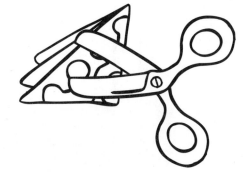 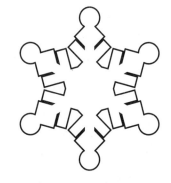

UNIT 10

Name:_____

Sequence Words

Directions: First, **next**, **then**, and **finally** are sequence words. They tell when something happens. Read the story. Look at the pictures. Then, write the numbers 1, 2, 3, and 4 in the boxes to show the correct order of the story.

First, Ducky packed his things. Next, he went to the airport. Then, he landed. Finally, he was on the island.

Name:_____

Sequence Words

Directions: After is a sequence word. It tells when something happens. Circle the picture in each row that shows what happened after the first two pictures.

Sequencing   241   © 2007 School Specialty Publishing

UNIT 10

Name:_____

Words About Living in the Country

Directions: Look at the picture. Use the words in the Word Bank to tell what you think it would be like to live in the country. Then, trace and write the word.

Word Bank				
plants	trees	hills	road	frog

country

Name:_____

Words About the Human Body

Directions: Use the words in the Word Bank to complete the picture. Then, color the picture.

Word Bank					
head	neck	arms	hands	legs	feet

Name:_____

Words About the Human Body

Directions: This is Norman. Use the picture to answer the questions about Norman.

How many hands does Norman have?

_____

- - - - - - - - - - - - - - - - - - -

_____

How many feet does Norman have?

_____

- - - - - - - - - - - - - - - - - - -

_____

How many legs does Norman have?

_____

- - - - - - - - - - - - - - - - - - -

_____

Name:_____

Words About the Human Body

Directions: Look at each picture. Which body part is each person using? Draw lines to match the words to the correct pictures.

mouth

legs

UNIT 10

Name:_____

Words About Fractions

Directions: Look at each shape. Color each half a different color. Then, trace and write the word.

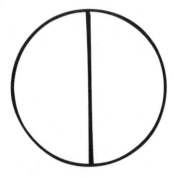
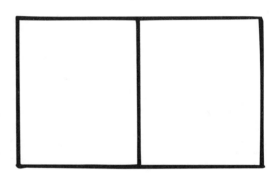

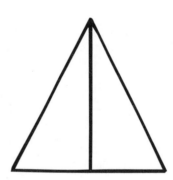

half -

Name:_____

Sequence Words

Directions: Cut out the pictures. Then, put each set in order to show what happens. Use the words **first**, **next**, and **last** to talk about the pictures.

UNIT 10

Page left blank for cutting activity.

Name:_____

Sequence Words

Directions: After is a sequence word. It tells when something happens. Look at the first two pictures. Then, circle the picture that shows what happened after.

Directions: First, **second**, **third**, and **fourth** are sequence words. Write the numbers 1, 2, 3, and 4 in the boxes above the pictures to show the correct order.

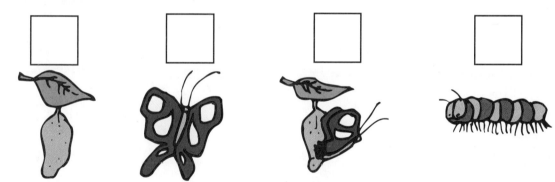

Directions: Next is a sequence word. Look at the first two pictures. Then, circle the picture that shows what will happen next.

UNIT 10

Name:_____

Words About Living by Water

Directions: Look at the picture. Use the words in the Word Bank to tell what you think it would be like to live by water. Then, trace and write the word.

Word Bank

water   lake   insects   plants   animals   boat   row

water

Name:_____

Words About the Human Body

Directions: Trace and write the words.

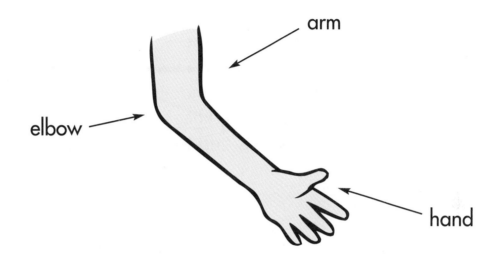

arm

elbow

hand

arm

elbow

hand

UNIT 10

Name:_____

Words About the Human Body

Directions: Sing the song. Point to each body part as you sing about it.

Head, shoulders, knees, and toes,
knees and toes.
Head, shoulders, knees, and toes,
knees and toes.
Eyes and ears and mouth and nose.
Head, shoulders, knees, and toes,
knees and toes!

UNIT 10

Name:_____

Words About the Human Body

Directions: Draw a picture of yourself from head to toe. Label each body part.

UNIT 10

Name:_____

Unit 10 Review

Directions: Pretend that you are buying a pet. Draw pictures to show what you would do first, next, and last. Talk about your pictures.

Directions: Draw a picture of the community where you live. Label your picture **city** or **country**.

Language Arts Words:
Reading 256–257
Parts of a Book 258, 264–265
Genre...266, 272–274

Social Studies Words:
Celebrations 259, 267, 275

Science Words:
Landforms...260–262, 268
Habitats 269–270, 276–278

Math Words:
Time..263, 271

Unit 11 Review 279

Name:_____

Words in Print

Words are everywhere! They are in books, in newspapers, and even on globes.

Directions: Draw a line from the item on the left to the same item on the right. Then, color the things that are made of paper.

A Big
Bug

Mom
and
Me

Mom
and
Me

A Big
Bug

UNIT 11

Name:_____

Words in Print

Directions: Color the pictures of things you can read. Then, trace and write the word.

BOOK

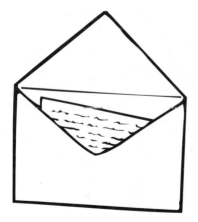

read

Name:_____

Words in Print

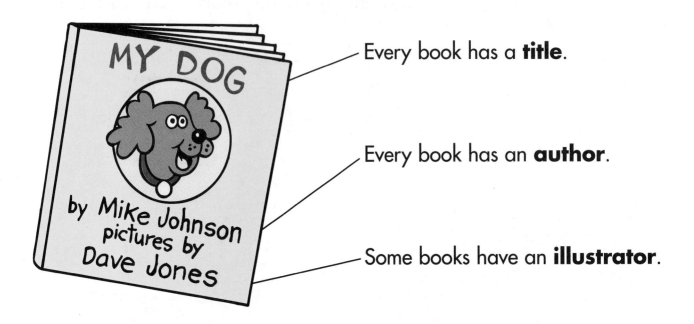

Every book has a **title**.

Every book has an **author**.

Some books have an **illustrator**.

Directions: Draw a line to match each word to the part of the book it names.

illustrator

title

author

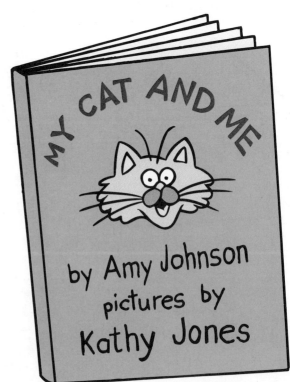

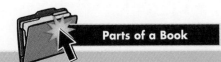

 UNIT 11

Name:_____

Words About Landforms

Directions: Mountains, lakes, canyons, and **rivers** are landforms. Draw lines to match the words that are the same. Point to the parts of picture that the words name.

mountain   **river**

lake   **lake**

canyon   **canyon**

river   **mountain**

Landforms   **261**

UNIT 11

Name:_____

Words About Landforms

Directions: Lakes and **forests** are landforms. Use the words in the Word Bank to complete the letter. Then, circle the two words in the Word Bank that are landforms.

Word Bank	
lake	six
pancakes	forest

Dear Mom and Dad,

_____

I woke up at _____ o'clock and got

_____

dressed. My friends and I ate _____ for

_____

breakfast. We went hiking in the _____ .

_____

Then, we went swimming in the _____ .

Camp is fun!

Love,
Kate

UNIT 11

Name:_____

Time Words

Directions: A **clock** is the best way to tell time. There are many kinds of clocks. Circle the ones you have seen.

cuckoo clock

watch

pocket watch

alarm clock

8:00

digital clock

grandfather clock

Name:_____

Words in Print

Directions: Every story has a title. Read the title of each story. Color the books. Then, trace and write the word.

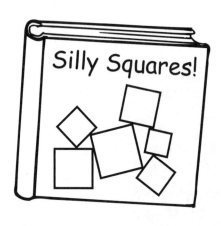

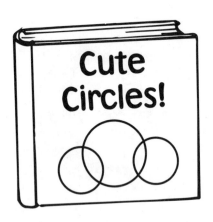

title

Parts of a Book

264

Name:_____

Words in Print

Directions: Read the poem. Then, answer the questions.

Mom reads *Silly Puppy*.
That's my favorite book.
It has great illustrations.
I listen and I look!

What is the title of the book? _____

_____

What are the pictures of a book called? _____

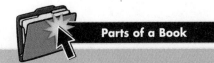
UNIT 11

Name:_____

Words About Genre

Directions: A **fairy tale** is a kind of story. *The Gingerbread Man* and *Goldilocks and the Three Bears* are fairy tales. Color the picture from each story. Then, trace and write the words.

The Gingerbread Man

Goldilocks and the Three Bears

fairy tale

UNIT 11

Name:_____

Celebration Words

Directions: Circle each picture that shows a birthday word. Then, draw something else you would see at a birthday party.

balloons

gift

hat

zipper

UNIT 11

Name:_____

Words About Landforms

Directions: An **ocean** is a landform. Many animals live in the ocean. Trace and write the word. Then, draw a picture of the ocean and some of the animals that live there.

ocean

© 2007 School Specialty Publishing

Name:_____

Habitat Words

Directions: A **habitat** is a home. A sea turtle's habitat is the sea. **Sea** and **ocean** mean the same thing. Trace and write the word. Then, draw a line to follow the path from the sea turtle to the ocean.

sea

Name:_____

Habitat Words

Directions: The swan's habitat is a lake. Trace and write the word.
Connect the dots from 1 to 10. Then, color the picture.

lake

UNIT 11

Name:_____

Time Words

Directions: A clock has different parts. Read the words. Trace the parts. Then, color the hands.

Numbers   **Face**

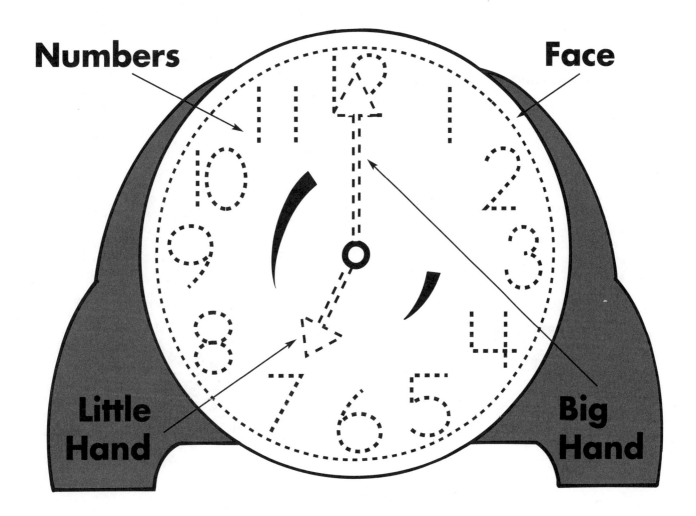

Little Hand   **Big Hand**

The **big hand** tells the minute.
The **little hand** tells the hour.

UNIT 11

Name:_____

Words About Genre

Directions: Read the story about the ant and the lion. Then, answer the question.

Once upon a time, there was an ant and a lion. The lion gave the ant three wishes. The ant's first wish was to ride an elephant. The ant's second wish was to ride an alligator. The ant's last wish was for three more wishes.

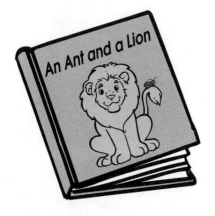

Is this story **real** or **fantasy**? _____

UNIT 11

Name:_____

Words About Genre

Directions: Draw a line to show if each book is real or fantasy.

Real   **Fantasy**

UNIT 11

Name: _____

Words About Genre

Directions: Fantasy stories are not real. **Real** stories actually happened. Draw an **X** on each thing in the picture that is not real. There are ten.

UNIT 11

Genres

274

© 2007 School Specialty Publishing

WEEK 33 language arts

Name: _____

Celebration Words

Directions: A **picnic** is a summertime celebration. Connect the dots from 1 to 10. Color the picture. Then, trace and write the word.

picnic

Name:_____

Habitat Words

Directions: Draw a line from each animal to its habitat. Then, say the name of the habitat.

cat

fish

squirrel

horse

bird

house

nest

tree

barn

lake

UNIT 11

Name:_____

Habitat Words

Directions: Whales and walruses live in the ocean. Trace and write the words.

whale

walrus

ocean

Name:_____

Habitat Words

Directions: Circle the animal whose habitat is a cave. Then, write its name on the line.

_____

- -

Name:_____

Unit 11 Review

Directions: Use the words in the Word Bank to write a story about a birthday party. Ask an adult to help you. Be sure to give your story a title.

Word Bank					
hat	gifts	cake	balloons	house	book

title

UNIT 11

UNIT 12

Language Arts Words:
Story Elements................281–283, 289–291, 297–299

Social Studies Words:
United States 284, 292, 300

Science Words:
Water 285–287, 293–295, 301–303

Math Words:
Money...288, 296

Unit 11 Review..304

Name:_____

Story Words

Directions: Every story has a **character**. A character thinks and talks. A character can even be a talking animal! Draw a line from each character to what it might say.

"I save lots of bones and bury them in the yard."

"I live in the ocean and have sharp teeth."

"I love to walk in the snow and slide on the ice."

"I hop on lily pads in a pond with my webbed feet."

"I slither on the ground because I have no arms or legs."

Story Elements

281

UNIT 12

Name:_____

Story Words

Directions: A story has a **plot**. The plot is everything that happens in the story. Look at the pictures in each row. Write 1, 2, and 3 in the boxes to show what happened first, second, and third in each story's plot.

Name:_____

Story Words

The **setting** tells when and where a story happens.

Directions: Read the story. Then, answer the questions.

It is snowing. My brother and I go outside to play. We build a snowman. Now, it is time for lunch. We go inside. It has been a fun morning!

_____

When does the story happen? _____

_____

Where does the story happen? _____

Name:_____

Words About the United States

This is the United States of America's flag. It has 50 stars, 7 red stripes, and 6 white stripes.

Directions: Use the words in the Word Bank to describe the American flag.

Word Bank		
red	white	blue
stars	stripes	flag

Words About Water

Directions: Ice is frozen water. Take an ice cube from the freezer. Place it in the sun. Answer the question below.

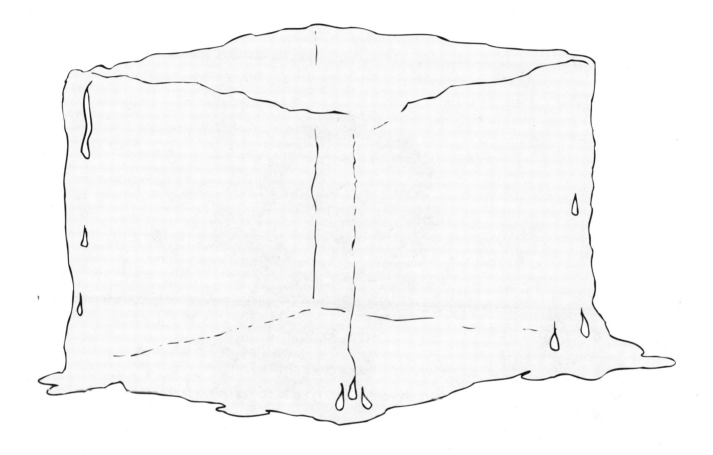

What does the ice do in the sun? _____

Matter

© 2007 School Specialty Publishing

UNIT 12

Name:_____

Words About Water

Directions: Water is wet. Trace the word.

Name:_____

Words About Water

Water can take different forms. Ice and snow are forms of water. Steam is a form of water, too.

Directions: Circle the picture that answers each question.

Which picture shows water as ice?

Which picture shows water as snow?

Which picture shows water as steam?

UNIT 12

Money Words

Directions: A **penny**, a **nickel**, and a **dime** are **coins**. Coins are a form of money. Look at the coins. Then, trace and write the words.

penny

nickel

dime

penny

nickel

dime

Name:_____

Story Words

Directions: Use the questions to help tell a story about the picture.

Who is the main character?

What is the setting?

What is the plot?

Name:_____

Words About the United States

Directions: Here is a map of the United States. Circle the state in which you live. Write the name of your state to complete the sentence.

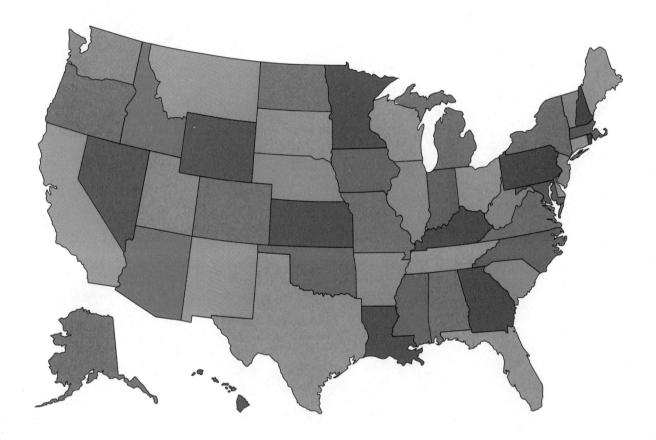

I live in the state of _____.

Name:_____

Words About Water

Directions: These three children are ready to play with water in its different forms. Use the words in the Word Bank to tell two sentences about each child.

Word Bank		
pool	snow	rain
cold	hot	melt

Name:_____

Words About Water

Directions: The ice cream will melt if you don't eat it fast! Draw ten sprinkles on the ice cream. Trace the word.

melt

Name:_____

Words About Water

Directions: Color the raindrops blue that have water words in them.

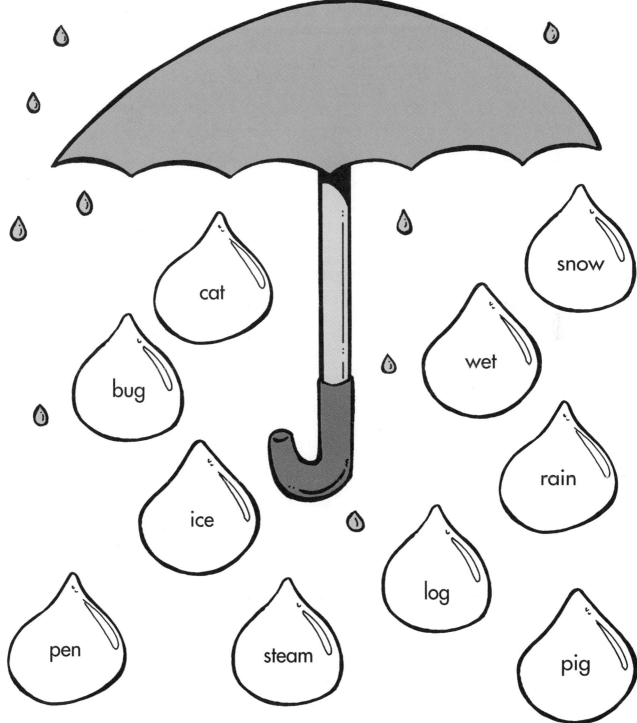

UNIT 12

Name:_____

Money Words

Directions: Follow the steps 1 through 3 to complete the picture.

1. Color all the **pennies** in the bank brown.
2. Color all the **nickels** in the bank red.
3. Color all the **dimes** in the bank blue.

penny

nickel

dime

UNIT 12

Name:_____

Story Words

Directions: Do you know the story of *Goldilocks and the Three Bears*? This house belongs to the bears. It is the setting of the story. Draw Goldilocks. She is a character in the story. Color the picture. Then, trace the words.

setting   character

Name:_____

Story Words

The **plot** of a story tells what happened.

Directions: Read the sentence. Ask and adult to help you write two sentences that tell what happened next. Then, draw a picture to match the plot of your story.

Sally went to the shelter to choose a new pet.

© 2007 School Specialty Publishing

Name:_____

Story Words

Directions: Draw a picture of the main character in your favorite story.

UNIT 12

Name:_____

Words About the United States

The **president** is the leader of the United States. **George Washington** was the first president. He is called "the father of our country." Here is his picture.

Directions: Color the picture of George Washington.

Name:_____

Words About Water

Directions: Use the words in the Word Bank to write the answers to the riddles. Then, draw the answers.

Word Bank		
ocean	watermelon	soap

I am a fruit.
I am red inside.
Water is in my name.
What am I?

_____

- - - - - - - - - - - - - - - -

I am a body of water.
I am salty.
I am home to many fish.
What am I?

- - - - - - - - - - - - - - - -

Use me with water.
I make suds.
I help you get clean.
What am I?

- - - - - - - - - - - - - - - -

Water

301

© 2007 School Specialty Publishing

UNIT 12

Words About Water

Think of all the ways you use water at home. You can use water to wash many things, including a dog!

Directions: Circle the word that completes each sentence. Then, write the word on the line.

1. Today, we will _____ our dog.

                            wash   cry

2. We will use _____ to make sure he gets clean!

                      sap   soap

3. We need _____ to rinse him off.

                  water   dirt

4. We will get the water from a _____.

                           plant   hose

Name:_____

Words About Water

Directions: Water comes in different forms. Look at the picture. The teacup contains hot water. Draw steam coming from the tea. Draw three ice cubes on the table. Draw a puddle on the floor. Then, color the picture.

UNIT 12

Unit 12 Review

Directions: Draw a line to match each word to its description.

character   everything that happens in a story

ice   a coin

plot   the person in a story

setting   something with 50 stars and red and white stripes

penny   when and where a story happens

American flag   frozen water

UNIT 12

Direction Words

Directions: The word **left** tells a direction. Look at the picture. Trace the word.

left

6

Direction Words

Directions: The word **right** tells a direction. Look at the picture. Trace the word.

right

7

Direction Words

Directions: The words **left** and **right** tell direction. Color the pictures on the left blue. Color the pictures on the right red. Then, write the correct direction word under each picture.

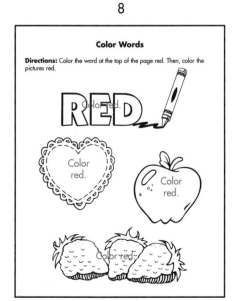

Color blue.   Color red.

left   right

Color blue.   Color red.

left   right

8

Words About Me

Directions: Write your name. Then, draw a picture of yourself doing something you like.

Pictures will vary.

9

Color Words

Directions: Color the word at the top of the page red. Then, color the pictures red.

RED — Color red.

Color red.   Color red.

Color red.

10

Color Words

Directions: Color the word at the top of the page orange. Then, color the pictures orange.

ORANGE — Color orange.

Color orange.   Color orange.

Color orange.

11

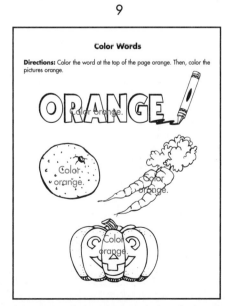

Color Words

Directions: Color the word at the top of the page yellow. Then, color the pictures yellow.

12

Number Words

Directions: Trace and write the word. Then, draw an **X** on each tank that has zero fish.

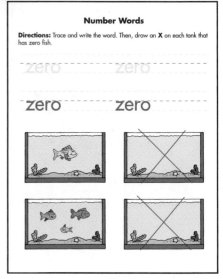

13

Direction Words

Directions: Trace the lines from left to right to help each mother find her baby.

14

Direction Words

Directions: Draw a line from the picture on the left to the picture on the right in each row.

15

Direction Words

Directions: The word **top** tells you **where**. Look at the picture. Trace the word.

16

Words About Me

Directions: Write your address. Then, draw a picture of where you live.

Answers will vary.

Pictures will vary.

17

Color Words

Directions: Color the word at the top of the page green. Then, color the pictures green.

GREEN
Color green.
Color green.
Color green.
Color green.

18

Color Words

Directions: Color the word at the top of the page blue. Then, color the pictures blue.

BLUE
Color blue.
Color blue.
Color blue.
Color blue.

19

Color Words

Directions: Color the word at the top of the page purple. Then, color the pictures purple.

PURPLE
Color purple.
Color purple.
Jam
Color purple.
Color purple.

20

Number Words

Directions: Trace and write the words. Then, count the number of things in each box. Write the correct number word on the line.

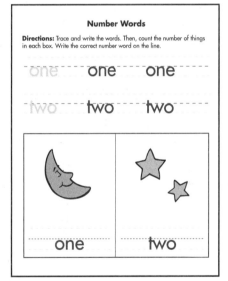

one   one   one
two   two   two

one | two

21

Direction Words

Directions: The word **bottom** tells you **where**. Look at the picture. Trace the word.

bottom

22

Direction Words

Directions: Trace the lines from top to bottom to help the girl paint the fence.

23

307

Direction Words

Directions: Trace the lines from top to bottom to help the spiders make their web.

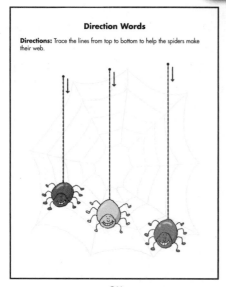

24

Words About Me

Directions: Follow steps 1 and 2 to draw a picture of yourself.
1. Draw and color your face and hair.
2. Draw and color the clothes you wear.

Pictures will vary.

25

Color Words

Directions: Color the word at the top of the page black. Then, color the pictures black.

BLACK

Color black.
Color black.
Color black.
Color black.

26

Color Words

Directions: Color the word at the top of the page brown. Then, color the pictures brown.

BROWN

Color brown.
Color brown.
Color brown.
Color brown.

27

Color Words

Directions: Use the color words in the flowers to color the picture.

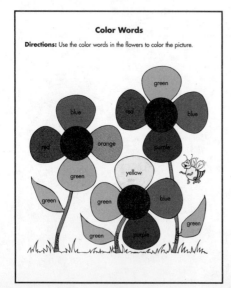

green
blue red blue
red orange
green purple
yellow
green blue
green green
green purple

28

Unit 1 Review

Directions: Find the two things in each row that are the same color. Color them with the correct crayon. Then, circle the things on the left. Draw an X on the things on the right.

Color black. Color black.
Color red. Color red.
Color orange. Color orange.

29

ANSWER key

Words That Name Things

Directions: Draw a line to match each word to its picture.

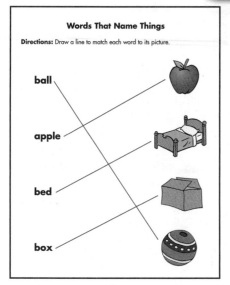

- ball
- apple
- bed
- box

31

Words That Name Things

Directions: Draw a line to match each word to its picture.

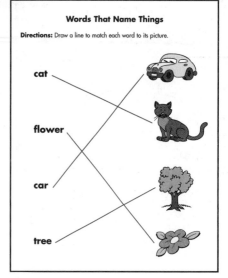

- cat
- flower
- car
- tree

32

Words That Name Things

Directions: Draw a line to match each word to its picture.

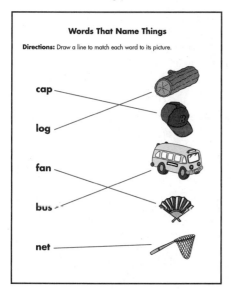

- cap
- log
- fan
- bus
- net

33

Words About Family

Directions: Draw a line to match each word to its picture.

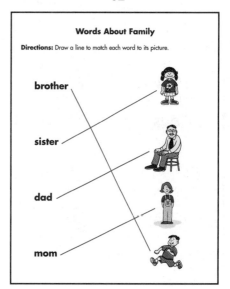

- brother
- sister
- dad
- mom

34

Animal Words

Directions: Trace each animal name. Draw a ball for each animal. Then, color the pictures.

seal   cat

dog   dolphin

35

309

Animal Words

Directions: Name each picture. Then, write the correct letter at the beginning of each word.

hen   cat

dog   rat

36

Animal Words

Directions: Draw lines from the word **swim** to the animals that swim. Draw lines from the word **fly** to the animals that fly.

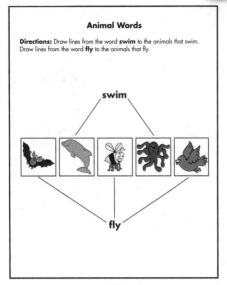

swim

fly

37

Number Words

Directions: Trace and write the words. Then, count the number of things in each box. Write the correct number word on the line.

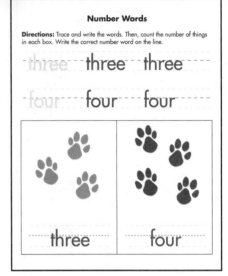

three three three

four four four

three | four

38

Words That Name Things

Directions: Circle the word that names each picture. Then, write the word on the line.

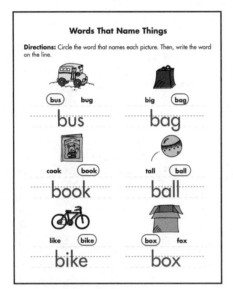

(bus) bug | big (bag)

bus | bag

cook (book) | tall (ball)

book | ball

like (bike) | (box) fox

bike | box

39

Words That Name Things

Directions: Name each picture. Then, write the letter to complete each word.

ham | jar

rug | pig

40

Words That Name Things

Directions: Read the words in the Word Bank. Then, write each word on the correct line.

Word Bank

pig	Kim	dog	blue
red	green	ten	five
Jack	two	cow	Lee

Name Words

Jack Kim Lee

Number Words

two ten five

Animal Words

pig dog cow

Color Words

red green blue

41

Words About Family

Directions: Look at the picture below. Trace the word. Then, write a sentence about your family. Ask an adult for help.

family

Sentences will vary.

42

310

Animal Words

Directions: Trace and write the animal words.

frog frog frog
fish fish fish
fox fox fox

43

Animal Words

Directions: Look at the picture of each animal. Write the letter **a**, **e**, **i**, **o**, or **u** to finish each word.

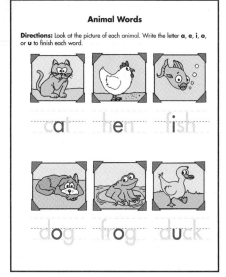

c**a**t h**e**n f**i**sh

d**o**g fr**o**g d**u**ck

44

Animal Words

Directions: Find and circle the animal words in the puzzle. Look across and down.

b	a	t	h	c	i	t
x	c	c	g	o	k	f
a	y	a	p	o	n	i
r	a	t	j	m	p	l
n	r	i	p	i	g	n

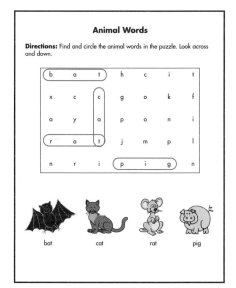

bat   cat   rat   pig

45

Number Words

Directions: Trace and write the words. Then, count the number of things in each box. Write the correct number word on the line.

five five five
six six six

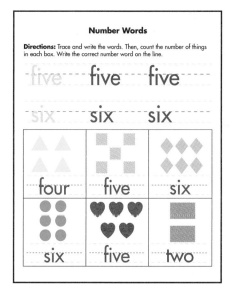

| four | five | six |
| six | five | two |

46

Words That Name Things

Directions: Name each picture. Then, write the correct letter to finish the word.

ball   mop   cup

bed   cap   pan

47

Words That Name Places

Directions: Read the story. Then, circle the words that name places.

Heads for Boston!
Tails for Portland!

Over a hundred years ago, two men built a (town) They couldn't decide what to name it. One man wanted to call it (Boston) The other wanted to name it (Portland) They tossed a coin and one yelled, "Heads for (Boston!)" The other yelled, "Tails for (Portland)" Tails must have won because that (town) is now called (Portland, Oregon)

48

ANSWER key

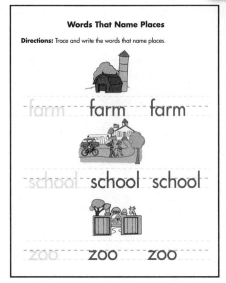

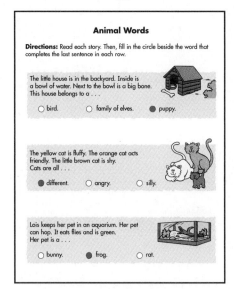

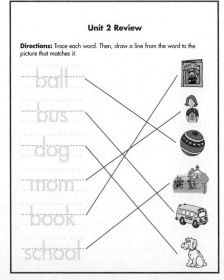

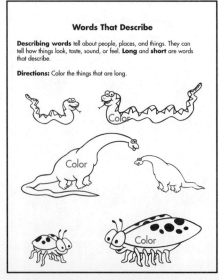

312

ANSWER key

Words That Describe

Directions: Color the things that are short.

57

Words That Describe

Directions: Tall is a word that describes. Color the people who are tall.

58

School Words

Directions: Look at the pictures. Then, trace and write the words.

pen   pen   pen

desk   desk   desk

59

Words About Farm Animals

Directions: Draw a line between the fences to help the lamb get back to the barn.

lamb

barn

60

Words About Farm Animals

Directions: Draw an **X** on the animal that does not belong on the farm. Then, color the animals that do belong.

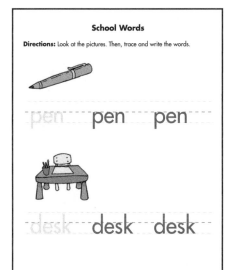

seal   Color   horse
Color   duck   pig

61

313

Words About Farm Animals

Directions: Draw a line to match each baby farm animal to the parent farm animal. Then, color the pictures.

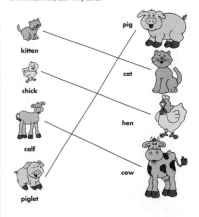

kitten   pig
chick   cat
calf   hen
piglet   cow

62

Number Words

Directions: Trace and write the words. Then, count the number of things in each box. Write the correct number word on the line.

seven seven seven

eight eight eight

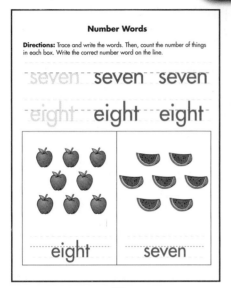

eight | seven

63

Words That Describe

Directions: Big and small are describing words. Color the big pictures yellow. Color the small pictures green.

64

Words That Describe

Directions: Circle the picture that shows something small. Then, color the picture.

Directions: Circle the picture that shows something big. Then, color the picture.

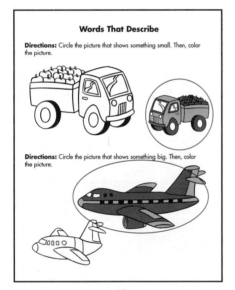

65

Words That Describe

Directions: Draw a line to match each word to the picture it describes.

tall

short

old

big

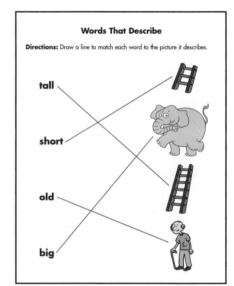

66

Words About Home

Directions: Follow the steps 1 through 3 to complete the picture.

1. Draw a bathtub and sink in the bathroom.
2. Draw a bed and rug in the bedroom.
3. Draw a refrigerator and toaster in the kitchen.

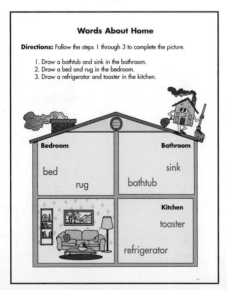

Bedroom — bed, rug
Bathroom — sink, bathtub
Kitchen — toaster, refrigerator

67

Words About Farm Animals

Directions: Look at each picture. Then, trace the word. At the bottom, write a sentence about farm animals. Ask an adult for help.

horse
cow
pig
chicken

Sentences will vary.

68

Words About Farm Animals

Directions: Make a memory game. Cut out the cards and place them facedown. Play the game with a partner. Take turns turning over the cards to match each mother farm animal with the correct baby farm animal.

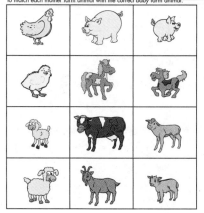

69

Number Words

Directions: Trace and write the words. Then, count the number of things in each box. Write the correct number word on the line.

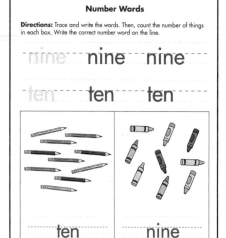

nine   nine   nine

ten   ten   ten

ten   nine

71

Words That Describe

Directions: Color the small pictures green. Color the big pictures orange.

Color orange.

Color green.

Color green.   Color orange.

72

Words That Describe

Directions: Draw a line to match each word to the picture it describes.

little

happy

sad

funny

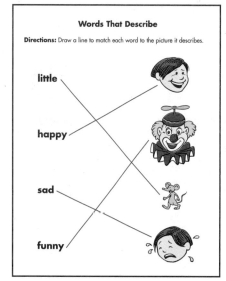

73

Words That Describe

Directions: Color the picture in each row that both words describe.

soft and **cold**

tall and **sad**

hot and **hard**

74

Words About Home

Directions: When someone comes home after being away, you say, "Welcome home." Trace the words. Then, draw a picture of your home.

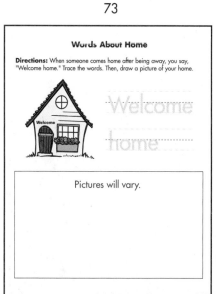

Welcome

home

Pictures will vary.

75

315

Words About Zoo Animals

Directions: Color the animals that live at the zoo.

lion   zebra

lamb   giraffe

76

Words About Zoo Animals

Directions: Help the zebra find its way to the zoo. Color the boxes from **A** to **Z**. Then, circle and name the other zoo animal in the picture.

77

Words About Zoo Animals

Directions: Draw a line from each riddle to the picture that answers it.

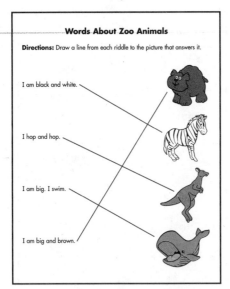

I am black and white.

I hop and hop.

I am big. I swim.

I am big and brown.

78

Unit 3 Review

Directions: Use a word from the Word Bank to complete each sentence.

Word Bank						
sink	cow	small	happy	desk	big	ten

1. I sit at a ___desk___ when I am at school.

2. A ___cow___ lives on a farm.

3. The number ___ten___ comes after the number nine.

4. A piglet is ___small___. Its mother is ___big___.

5. I wash my hands in the ___sink___.

6. I am ___happy___ when I play with my friends.

79

Action Words

Directions: An **action word** tells what a person or thing does. Draw a line to match each action word to the person doing the action.

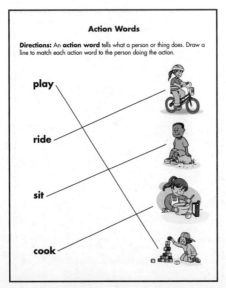

play

ride

sit

cook

81

316

Action Words

Directions: Draw a line to match each action word to the person or people doing the action.

walk

run

talk

eat

82

ANSWER key

Action Words

Directions: Write the letter that completes each action word. Then, color the pictures.

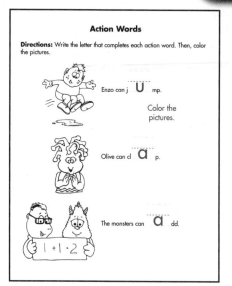

Enzo can j **u** mp.

Color the pictures.

Olive can cl **a** p.

The monsters can **a** dd.

83

Transportation Words

Directions: Circle the things that have wheels.

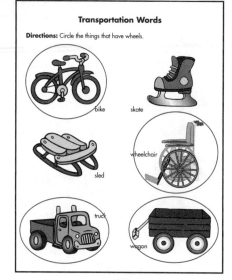

bike · skate · sled · wheelchair · truck · wagon

84

Insect Words

Directions: Trace and write the insect word. Then, draw eight legs on each spider.

spider spider
spider spider

85

Insect Words

Directions: Write each insect word on the line. Then, draw another fly and another bee.

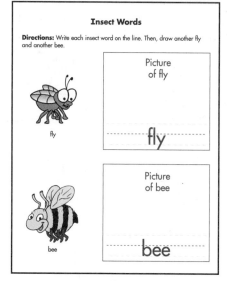

Picture of fly — **fly**

Picture of bee — **bee**

86

Insect Words

Directions: Read the insect words. Draw a line from each word to the part it names in the picture.

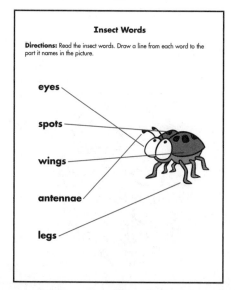

eyes
spots
wings
antennae
legs

87

Number Words

Directions: Count the beads on each string. Write the correct number word on the line.

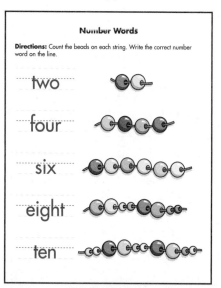

two
four
six
eight
ten

88

317

Action Words

Directions: Circle the action word that completes each sentence. Then, write the word on the line.

digs   wigs

Pup **digs** in the mud.

steps   naps

Pup **steps** on the rug.

hugs   pets

Mom **hugs** Pup.

89

Action Words

Directions: Circle the word that completes each sentence. Then, write the word on the line.

Dot will **tap** the ball with her bat.
(tap) tip hop

The kids **tug** on the rope.
tip (tug) sit

Can Ben **hit** the pin?
tip (hit) lay

The men **dig** a hole.
run dip (dig)

Pat **put** the pot in the bin.
cut rip (put)

90

Action Words

Directions: Look at each picture. Trace the word that tells what each person does.

run   hug

eat   step

91

Transportation Words

Directions: Read the transportation words. Then, circle the things that travel in the air.

train   car   bus

airplane   ship   balloon

truck   bicycle   helicopter

92

Insect Words

Directions: Trace and write the insect word. Then, connect the dots to find out how many ladybugs there are in all. Color the ladybugs.

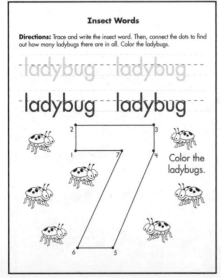

ladybug ladybug

ladybug ladybug

Color the ladybugs.

93

Insect Words

Directions: Draw eight spots on the ladybug. Then, point to the ladybug's antennae, head, eyes, and legs.

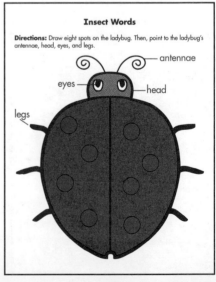

antennae

eyes   head

legs

94

318

Insect Words

Directions: Read about ladybugs. Then, answer the questions.

Ladybugs are red. They have black spots. They have six legs.

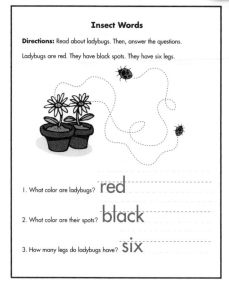

1. What color are ladybugs? red
2. What color are their spots? black
3. How many legs do ladybugs have? six

95

Number Words

Directions: Count the rabbits in each group. Then, draw a line to match each number to the word that tells how many.

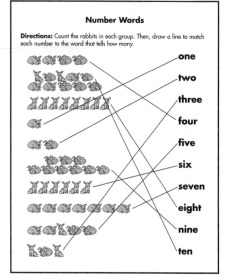

one
two
three
four
five
six
seven
eight
nine
ten

96

Action Words

Directions: Cut out the action words. Then, glue each word in the correct sentence.

1. The boy kicks the ball.
2. The hen sits in her nest.
3. I eat a sandwich.
4. She can jump a lot.
5. I can see you.

eat
jump
sits
kicks
run
see

97

Action Words

Directions: Color the flowers that have action words in them.

99

Transportation Words

Directions: Look at the pictures. Then, write the missing letter for each word.

bus van
truck sled

100

Insect Words

Directions: Look at the picture. Then, read the questions. Write the correct number word.

How many **butterflies** in all? three

How many **bees** in all? four

101

319

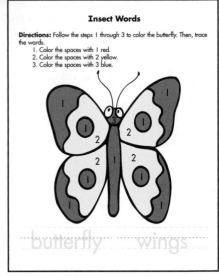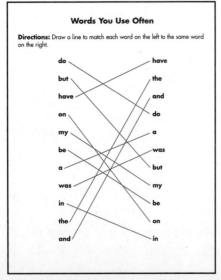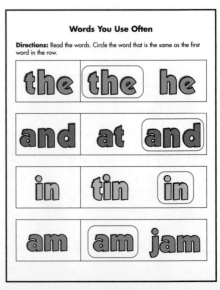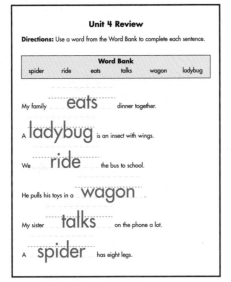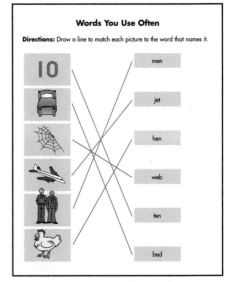

Insect Words

A **butterfly** is a type of insect. It has four wings.

Directions: Draw a line to connect the two matching butterflies.

102

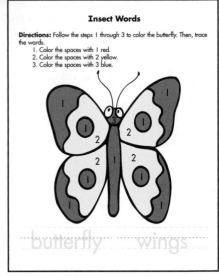

Insect Words

Directions: Follow the steps 1 through 3 to color the butterfly. Then, trace the words.
1. Color the spaces with 1 red.
2. Color the spaces with 2 yellow.
3. Color the spaces with 3 blue.

butterfly   wings

103

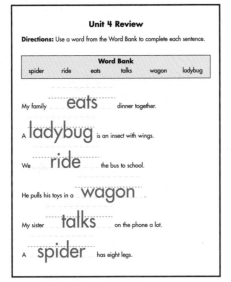

Unit 4 Review

Directions: Use a word from the Word Bank to complete each sentence.

Word Bank					
spider	ride	eats	talks	wagon	ladybug

My family **eats** dinner together.

A **ladybug** is an insect with wings.

We **ride** the bus to school.

He pulls his toys in a **wagon**.

My sister **talks** on the phone a lot.

A **spider** has eight legs.

104

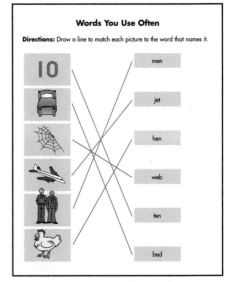

Words You Use Often

Directions: Draw a line to match each picture to the word that names it.

men

jet

hen

web

ten

bed

106

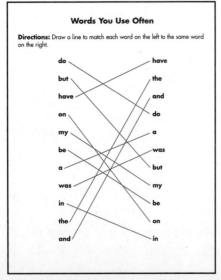

Words You Use Often

Directions: Draw a line to match each word on the left to the same word on the right.

do   have
but   the
have   and
on   do
my   a
be   was
a   but
was   my
in   be
the   on
and   in

107

320

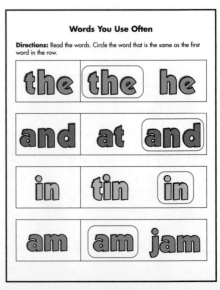

Words You Use Often

Directions: Read the words. Circle the word that is the same as the first word in the row.

the the he

and at and

in tin in

am am jam

108

Clothing Words

Directions: Color the pictures that are clothes.

shirt   coat

pants   car

109

Weather Words

Directions: Trace the word under each picture. Then, color the pictures.

sun   snow

cloud   rain

110

Weather Words

Directions: Cut out the cards. Match the things that go with sunny, rainy, and snowy weather.

sunny

rainy

snowy

111

Ordinal Number Words

Directions: Look at the train of animals. Then, write the word on the line that tells each animal's place in line.

first second third fourth fifth sixth seventh eighth ninth tenth

sixth   ninth

fifth   eighth

first   tenth

second   seventh

third   fourth

113

Words You Use Often

Directions: Read each word. Then, write it on the line.

look

do   but   look

do   but   look

the   had   he

the   had   he

of   I   on

of   I   on

to   my   all

to   my   all

114

321

Words You Use Often

Directions: Circle the two words in each row that are the same. The first one is done for you.

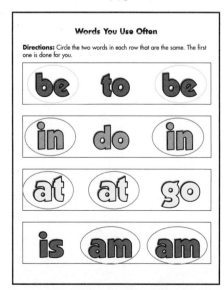

be   to   be

in   do   in

at   at   go

is   am   am

115

Words You Use Often

Directions: Look at each picture. Write the words from the Word Bank that finish each sentence. The first one is done for you.

Word Bank

fat	red	big
bed	pig	cat

The bed is red.

The pig is big.

The cat is fat.

116

Clothing Words

Directions: Look at the pictures of clothes. Trace the words. Then, read them aloud.

pants   sock

vest

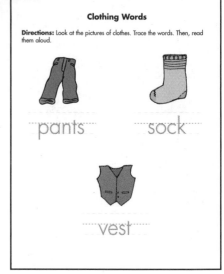

117

Weather Words

Directions: It is raining. This boy wants to play outside. Circle the things he needs to use to stay dry.

earmuffs

raincoat

umbrella

backpack

boots

skis

hat

118

Weather Words

Directions: You wear different things depending on the weather. Draw a picture to show what else you would wear for each type of weather.

Things for Warm Weather

Pictures will vary.

Things for Cold Weather

Things for Rainy Weather

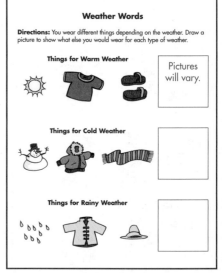

119

Weather Words

Directions: Read this story with an adult.

The itsy bitsy spider went up the water spout.

Down came the rain and washed the spider out.

Out came the sun and dried up all the rain.

And the itsy bitsy spider went up the spout again.

spider   up   water   spout

down   rain   sun

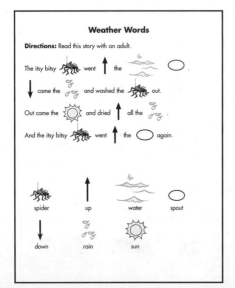

120

Ordinal Number Words

Directions: Follow steps 1 through 5 to complete the activity.
1. **Draw** a box around the **second** person in line.
2. **Draw** a line above the **fourth** person in line.
3. **Draw** an **X** on the **first** person in line.
4. **Draw** a line under the **fifth** person in line.
5. **Circle** the **third** person in line.

121

Words You Use Often

Directions: Write the word on the line that answers each riddle. Use the words at the bottom of the page.

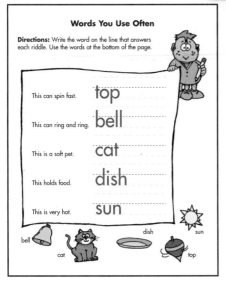

This can spin fast. **top**

This can ring and ring. **bell**

This is a soft pet. **cat**

This holds food. **dish**

This is very hot. **sun**

bell cat dish sun top

122

Words You Use Often

Directions: Cut out the cards. Read the words. Then, match each word to its picture.

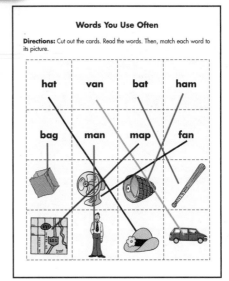

hat van bat ham

bag man map fan

123

Clothing Words

Directions: Look at all these hats! Trace and write the word. Then, draw a picture of a funny hat.

hat hat hat

Pictures will vary.

125

Weather Words

Directions: Connect the dots from 1 to 10. Answer the question at the bottom of the page. Then, color the picture.

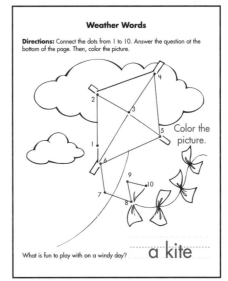

Color the picture.

What is fun to play with on a windy day? **a kite**

126

Weather Words

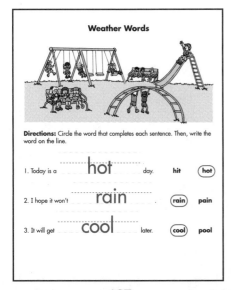

Directions: Circle the word that completes each sentence. Then, write the word on the line.

1. Today is a **hot** day.   hit   (hot)

2. I hope it won't **rain** .   (rain)   pain

3. It will get **cool** later.   (cool)   pool

127

Weather Words

Directions: Use the words in the Word Bank to complete the story.

Word Bank			
snow	ice	wind	cold

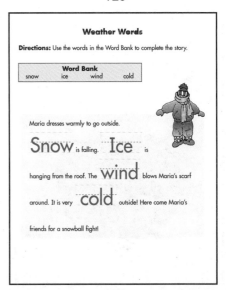

Maria dresses warmly to go outside.

Snow is falling. **Ice** is

hanging from the roof. The **wind** blows Maria's scarf

around. It is very **cold** outside! Here come Maria's

friends for a snowball fight!

128

323

Unit 5 Review

Directions: Use the Word Bank to find the word that is being described in each sentence. Write the word on the line.

Word Bank					
cat	coat	bed	sun	fifth	man

1. This shines on a hot, summer day.   sun

2. This is a popular pet.   cat

3. This number comes after fourth.   fifth

4. This is a grown-up boy.   man

5. You wear this when it is cold outside.   coat

6. You sleep in this.   bed

129

Position Words

Directions: On, **beside**, **under**, and **in** are position words. Follow steps 1 through 4 to complete the picture.

1. Draw a ladybug **on** the rock.
2. Draw a tree **beside** the rock.
3. Draw a butterfly **under** the birdbath.
4. Draw a bird **in** the birdbath.

131

Position Words

Directions: Between is a position word. Trace and color the cat that is between the other cats.

Directions: Color the mouse that is between the other mice.

132

Position Words

Directions: Over is a position word. Color the skunk that hit the ball over the grass.

133

Holiday Words

Valentine's Day is a holiday that happens every year on February 14. On this day, you think about the people you love, and you send them valentines.

Directions: Trace the words. Then, write the words on the heart. Color the heart.

I love you.

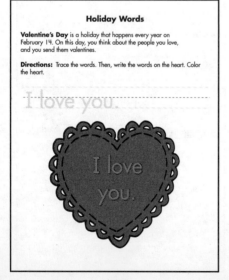

I love
you.

134

Winter Words

Directions: Color the pictures that show winter words.

snowman   watermelon

mitten   hat

135

ANSWER key

Winter Words

Directions: Circle the pictures that show winter words.

shell

boat

fish

sled

snowman

pail

136

Spring Words

Directions: Sometimes, it rains a lot in the spring. The rain helps flowers grow. Color the flowers. Then, trace and write the word.

Color the picture.

spring   spring

137

Shape Words

A **circle** is a round shape.

Directions: Trace the circles. Then, color the pictures.

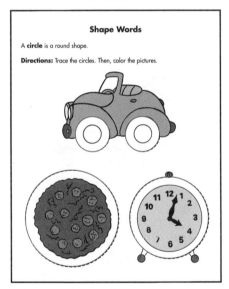

138

Position Words

Directions: Color and cut out the pictures at the bottom of the page. Then, glue them in the correct places.

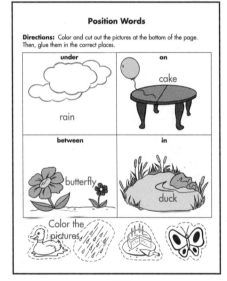

under

on

cake

rain

between

in

butterfly

duck

Color the pictures.

139

Position Words

Directions: **Above** and **below** are position words. Color the pictures above the clouds yellow. Then, color the pictures below the clouds blue.

141

325

Holiday Words

Thanksgiving is a holiday in November. On this day, you think about the things you are thankful for.

Directions: Trace the words. Color the picture. Then, use the words to tell about Thanksgiving.

thanks

Color

family

turkey

142

ANSWER key

Summer Words

Directions: Summer at the beach is fun! Follow steps 1 through 5 to complete the picture.
1. Color the umbrella yellow and purple.
2. Color the big beach ball red and blue.
3. Circle the boat.
4. Draw two blue fish in the water.
5. Draw a yellow sun in the sky.

143

Summer Words

Directions: Trace and write the summer words. Then, use the words to talk about the picture.

pool — pool
fun — fun
friends — friends
water — water

144

Summer Words

Directions: Look at the words and pictures. Then, draw two more pictures of summer things.

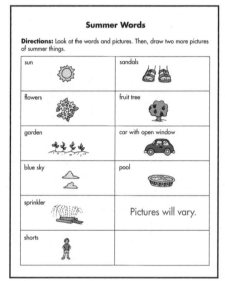

sun	sandals
flowers	fruit tree
garden	car with open window
blue sky	pool
sprinkler	Pictures will vary.
shorts	

145

Shape Words

A **square** is a shape with four equal sides.

Directions: Trace the word. Then, circle the square in each row.

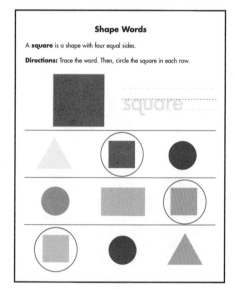

square

146

Position Words

Directions: **Above** and **below** are position words. Read the sentences. Draw a line to match each animal to its cage.
1. The lion goes below the monkey.
2. The tiger goes above the monkey.
3. The monkey goes above the lion and below the tiger.

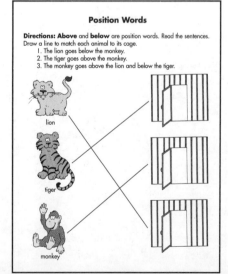

lion
tiger
monkey

147

Position Words

Directions: **Above** is a position word. Look at the picture. The sun is above the bird. Circle the other things above the bird.

148

326

ANSWER key

Position Words

Directions: Between is a position word. Find the shape in each row that is between the other shapes. Color it.

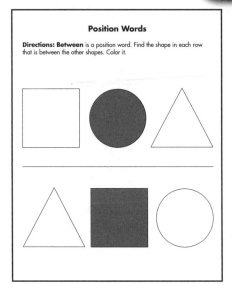

149

Holiday Words

Americans celebrate the **Fourth of July** every year. It is the birthday of the United States. Americans celebrate with parades and fireworks.

Directions: Trace the words. Then, use them to tell about the Fourth of July.

fireworks

parade

150

Fall Words

Directions: It is fun to rake the fall leaves! Color the leaves with **L** orange. Color the leaves with **I** red.

Color I red.
Color L orange.
Color I orange.
Color L orange.
Color I red.
Color I red.
Color I orange.
Color L orange.
Color I red.

151

Words About the Seasons

Directions: In the winter, it is cold outside. The daytime is short. Sometimes it snows. Color the children who are dressed for winter.

Directions: In the summer, it is warm outside. The daytime is long. The sun shines a lot. Color the children who are dressed for summer.

152

Words About the Seasons

Directions: Follow steps 1 through 4 to complete the pictures. Trace the words. Then, color the pictures.
1. **Draw** a rake in the picture of **fall**.
2. **Draw** a sled in the picture of **winter**.
3. **Draw** a butterfly in the picture of **spring**.
4. **Draw** a swimming pool in the picture of **summer**.

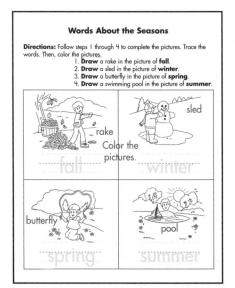

rake
Color the pictures.
fall
sled
winter
butterfly
spring
pool
summer

153

Unit 6 Review

Directions: Circle the position word in each sentence.

1. The dog hides (under) the table.

2. I sit (between) my two friends in class.

3. The ladybug sits (on) a rock.

4. The plane flies (over) the house.

Directions: Circle the season word described in each sentence.

The air is cool. Leaves are falling from the trees. We help rake them up.

winter   spring   summer   (fall)

The sun is bright and hot. We swim in the pool to cool off.

winter   spring   (summer)   fall

154

327

Words That Compare

Directions: **Same** and **different** are words that compare. Color the shape in each row that looks the same as the first shape.

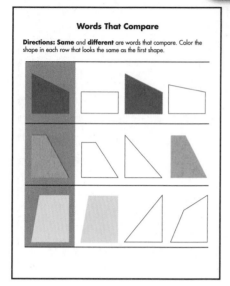

156

Words That Compare

Directions: **Taller** and **shorter** are words that compare two things. Circle the thing in each box that is taller than the other.

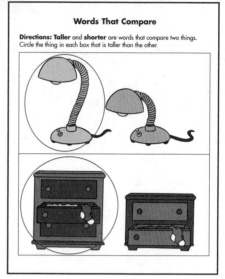

157

Words That Compare

Directions: **Longest** is a word that compares three or more things. Circle the longest thing in each row. The first one is done for you.

158

Job Words

Directions: Bob is a **baker**. A baker makes bread, cakes, and muffins. Circle the things Bob needs to do his job. At the bottom of the page, draw some treats from his bakery. Write the names of these treats.

Pictures and words will vary.

159

Time of Day Words

Directions: **Night** is the time when it is dark outside. Circle the things you usually do at night.

Directions: **Day** is the time when it is light outside. Draw a picture of something you do only in the day.

Pictures will vary.

160

Time of Day Words

Directions: Draw a picture of something in the night sky.

Pictures will vary.

day   night

Directions: Draw a picture of something you do at night.

Pictures will vary.

161

328

Time of Day Words

Directions: Look at the pictures. Then, trace the words. Read them aloud.

Good morning

Good night

162

Shape Words

A **rectangle** is a shape with two long sides and two short sides.

Directions: Trace the word. Then, color each rectangle the correct color.

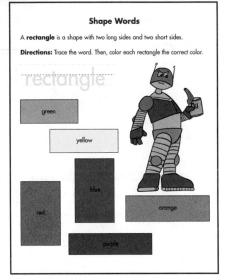

rectangle

163

Words That Compare

Directions: Shortest is a word that compares three or more things. Circle the shortest thing in each row. The first one is done for you.

164

Words That Compare

Directions: Color the longest thing in each row. Then, draw an **X** on the shortest thing in each row.

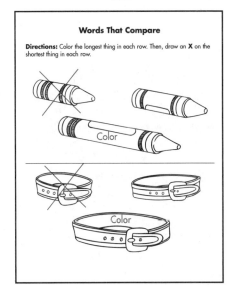

165

Words That Compare

Directions: Biggest and **smallest** are words that compare three or more things. Color the biggest thing in each row. Then, circle the smallest thing in each row.

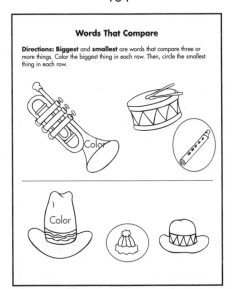

166

Job Words

Directions: Draw a line to match each person with the name of his or her job.

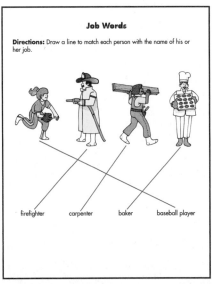

firefighter   carpenter   baker   baseball player

167

Time of Day Words

Directions: Color the things you see in the night sky.

moon   star

sun   balloon

168

Time of Day Words

Directions: Trace and write the word.

star   star   star

Directions: Circle the word **star** each time you read it in the poem.

Twinkle, twinkle little (star.)
How I wonder what you are.
Up above the world so high,
Like a diamond in the sky.
Twinkle, twinkle little (star.)
How I wonder what you are.

169

Space Words

Directions: Color each picture with the word **moon** or **star** in it.

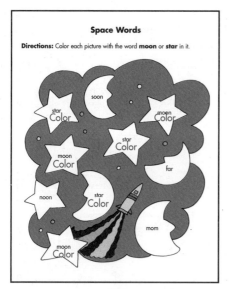

170

Shape Words

A **triangle** is a shape with three sides.

Directions: Trace the word. Then, color each triangle the correct color.

triangle

green   orange   brown   red   blue   yellow   purple

171

Words That Compare

Directions: **Shortest** is a word that compares three or more things. Color the shortest thing in each row. The first one is done for you.

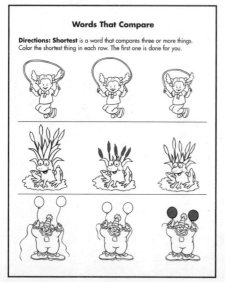

172

Words That Compare

Directions: **Smallest** and **biggest** are words that compare three or more things. Cut out the pictures. Then, put the animals in order from smallest to biggest.

173

Job Words

A **barber** cuts and styles hair. He works in a **barber shop**.

Directions: Circle the tools a barber might need. At the bottom of the page, draw something else he might need to do his job.

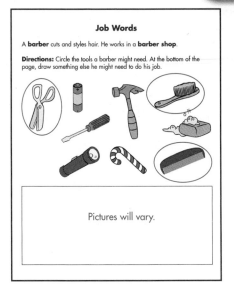

Pictures will vary.

175

Space Words

Word Bank

comet	moon	rocket	Mars	star	planet

Directions: Use the words in the Word Bank to find the rockets that contain space words. Then, color the rockets.

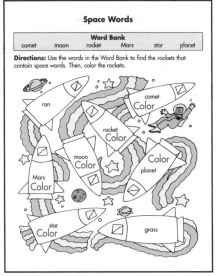

176

Space Words

Directions: Color the pictures of things you might find in space.

astronaut

moon

ant

rocket

177

Space Words

Directions: Trace and write the space words.

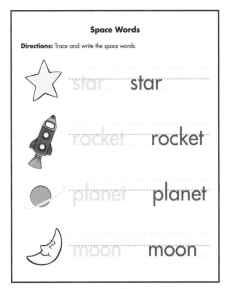

star   star

rocket   rocket

planet   planet

moon   moon

178

Unit 7 Review

Directions: Draw a line to match each word to its description.

day — when it is light outside

smallest — opposite of biggest

baker — someone who makes bread

star — something you see in the night sky

Directions: Draw each shape.

1. triangle

2. rectangle

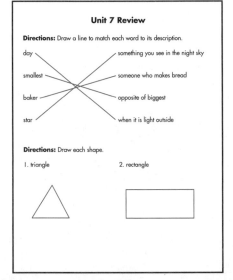

179

Words That Mean the Same Thing

Directions: Look at the pictures and the words that name them. Then, circle the word in each row that means the same thing as the first word.

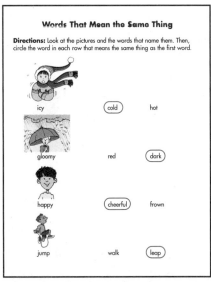

icy   (cold)   hot

gloomy   red   (dark)

happy   (cheerful)   frown

jump   walk   (leap)

181

331

Words That Mean the Same Thing

Directions: Read the sentences. Then, use the Word Bank to find the word that means the same thing as the word in blue. Write the word on the line.

Word Bank			
easy	right	huge	clean

1. The dinosaur is **huge** (big)

2. She keeps her room **clean** (tidy)

3. This math problem is **easy** (simple)

4. I got the **right** (correct) answer.

182

Words That Mean the Same Thing

Directions: Read each word. Find the word on the anthill that means the same thing. Then, write the word on the line.

1. glad **happy**
2. little **small**
3. begin **start**
4. above **over**
5. damp **wet**
6. large **big**

183

Words About Feelings

Directions: Read the words about feelings. Then, draw a picture of yourself when you are sad or happy.

sad   happy

Pictures will vary.

184

Plant Words

Directions: Read about plants. Then, answer the questions.

A plant grows from a seed.
A plant needs water and light to grow.
A plant can grow in a pot or in the ground.

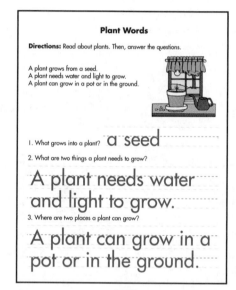

1. What grows into a plant? **a seed**

2. What are two things a plant needs to grow?
A plant needs water and light to grow.

3. Where are two places a plant can grow?
A plant can grow in a pot or in the ground.

185

Plant Words

Directions: Read about weeds. Then, answer the questions.

A **weed** is any plant that grows where people do not want it to grow. Weeds can grow fast. They make it harder for other plants to grow. The wind spreads the seeds from weeds. Birds and other animals also carry the seeds. Weeds are hard to get rid of.

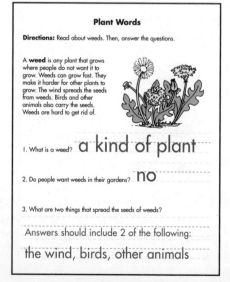

1. What is a weed? **a kind of plant**

2. Do people want weeds in their gardens? **no**

3. What are two things that spread the seeds of weeds?
Answers should include 2 of the following:
the wind, birds, other animals

186

Plant Words

Directions: Use the words in the Word Bank to write the parts of the plant.

Word Bank			
roots	stem	leaf	flower

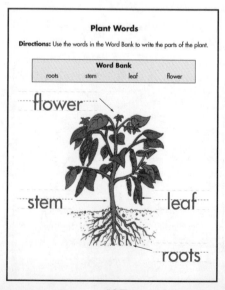

flower
stem
leaf
roots

187

332

Shape Words

A **star** is a shape with five points.

Directions: Trace and write the word. Then, draw five more stars in the picture.

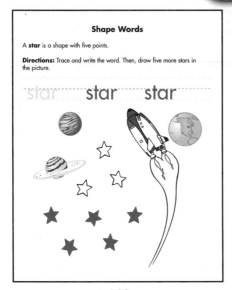

star   star   star

188

Words That Mean the Same Thing

Directions: Look at each picture and the word that describes it. Find a word in the Word Bank that is the same. Then, write the word on the line.

Word Bank				
afraid	tiny	loud	wet	warm

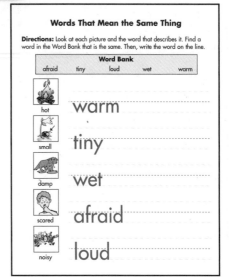

hot — warm
small — tiny
damp — wet
scared — afraid
noisy — loud

189

Words That Mean the Same Thing

Directions: Use the Word Bank to find the word that means the same thing as the underlined word in each sentence. Then, write the word on the line.

Word Bank			
sweet	fast	friend	rock

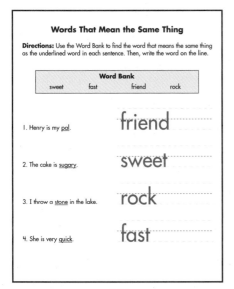

1. Henry is my pal. — friend
2. The cake is sugary. — sweet
3. I throw a stone in the lake. — rock
4. She is very quick. — fast

190

Words That Mean the Same Thing

Directions: There are many ways to tell how you feel. Look at each picture and the word that names it in the first column. Then, draw a line to match the words that are the same in the second column.

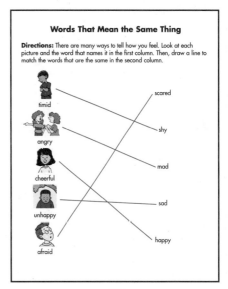

timid — shy
angry — mad
cheerful — happy
unhappy — sad
afraid — scared

191

Words About Feelings

Directions: Circle each happy face in the crowd. Then, trace the word on the balloon. Draw a happy face on the clown.

happy
Pictures will vary.

192

Plant Words

Directions: Fruits and vegetables come from plants. Color the fruits and vegetables. Then, name them.

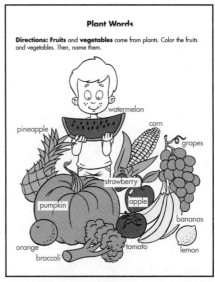

watermelon, pineapple, corn, grapes, strawberry, apple, pumpkin, bananas, orange, broccoli, tomato, lemon

193

333

Plant Words

Directions: **Flowers** are plants with petals, stems, and leaves. Draw the missing stems. Draw leaves on the stems. Then, color the flowers.

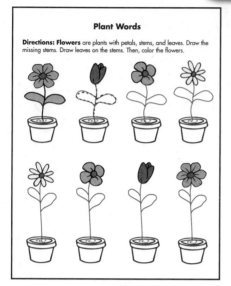

194

Plant Words

Lemons and **bananas** are fruit that grow on trees. **Corn** is a vegetable that grows up from the ground.

Directions: Draw something else that grows up from the ground. Then, color the pictures.

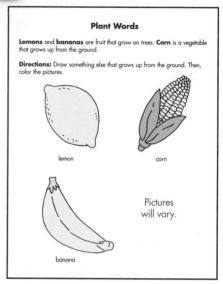

lemon

corn

Pictures will vary.

banana

195

Shape Words

Directions: Draw a line from each shape on the left to the shape that is the same on the right.

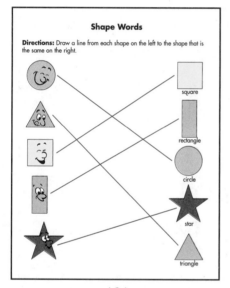

square

rectangle

circle

star

triangle

196

Words That Mean the Same Thing

Directions: Use the Word Bank to find the word that means the same thing as the underlined word in each sentence. Then, write the word.

Word Bank			
hog	tiny	throw	lady

1. A kitten is a <u>small</u> cat.   tiny

2. My mom is a <u>woman</u>.   lady

3. A <u>pig</u> lives on a farm.   hog

4. I <u>toss</u> the ball with my dad.   throw

197

Words That Mean the Same Thing

Directions: Draw a line to match each word on the left to the word on the right that means the same thing.

grin   boat

house   messy

dirty   home

good   smile

ship   nice

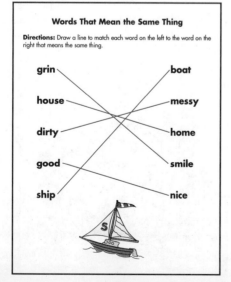

198

Words That Mean the Same Thing

Directions: Look at each picture. Then, write two words from the Word Bank that tell about each picture. The two words should mean the same thing.

Word Bank							
rocks	start	road	begin	street	stones	sad	unhappy

sad
unhappy

rocks
stones

road
street

start
begin

199

334

Words About Feelings

Directions: Look at each picture. Then, circle the word that tells what the animal or person is feeling.

- My tummy hurts. (sick) / well
- My hat is blowing away. (surprised) / angry
- I am seven years old today. (happy) / sad
- I can't find my home. silly / (scared)

200

Plant Words

Directions: Jack planted magic seeds. These seeds grew down, not up. Draw what Jack found when he followed his plant. Then, trace the words.

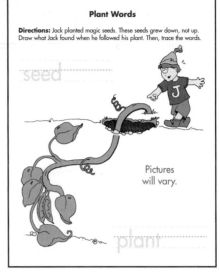

seed

Pictures will vary.

plant

201

Plant Words

Directions: First, Ben planted some seeds. Then, he watered the seeds. The sun shined on them. What happened next? Circle the correct picture. Then, trace and write the word.

flower **flower**

202

Plant Words

Directions: Gardening is fun! Color the picture. Then, circle the things that are named in the Word Bank.

Color the picture.

Word Bank
roots
leaves
rake
tree

203

Unit 8 Review

Directions: Draw lines to match the words that mean the same thing.

hot — warm
happy — glad
above — over
simple — easy
large — big
tiny — small

Directions: Use the words in the Word Bank to draw a picture of a plant. Then, label the plant parts.

Word Bank
seed
pot
flower
stem
leaf
roots

Pictures will vary. Check to see that parts of the plant are labeled correctly.

204

Words That Are Opposites

Directions: Opposites are things that are different in every way. Draw lines to match the opposites.

day — night
front — back
happy — sad
big — little

206

ANSWER key

Words That Are Opposites

Directions: Look at the word and picture in each row. Then, draw a picture of the opposite.

207

Words That Are Opposites

Directions: Look at the word and picture in each row. Then, draw a picture of the opposite.

208

Words About Friendship

Directions: Trace and write the words. Then, use the words to tell about the picture.

share share
friends friends
play play

209

Food Words

Directions: Draw a line to match each group of food to the meal it will make. Then, say the name of each finished meal.

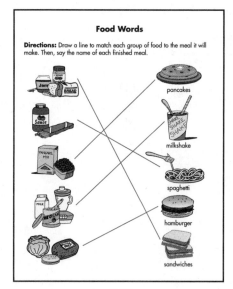

pancakes
milkshake
spaghetti
hamburger
sandwiches

210

Food Words

Directions: This hippo loves pizza! Pepperoni, mushrooms, and olives are its favorite toppings. Trace the dotted lines. Color the picture. Then, answer the question.

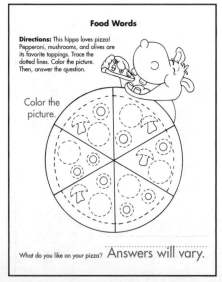

Color the picture.

What do you like on your pizza? Answers will vary.

211

Food Words

Directions: Crackers and pretzels are popular snack foods. Color the snack foods. Then, draw other snack foods that you like to eat.

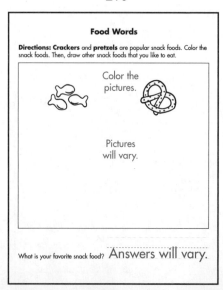

Color the pictures.

Pictures will vary.

What is your favorite snack food? Answers will vary.

212

Calendar Words

The days of the week are **Sunday**, **Monday**, **Tuesday**, **Wednesday**, **Thursday**, **Friday**, and **Saturday**. Saturday and Sunday make up the **weekend**.

Sunday 1	Monday 2	Tuesday 3	Wednesday 4	Thursday 5	Friday 6	Saturday 7

Directions: Look at the calendar above. Then, answer the questions.

1. Circle the first day of the week.
   (Sunday)   Monday   Thursday   Wednesday

2. Circle the last day of the week.
   Friday   (Saturday)

3. Which two days make up the weekend?

   Saturday   Sunday

4. Write the name of your favorite day of the week.

   Answers will vary.

213

Words That Are Opposites

Directions: Draw lines to match the opposites.

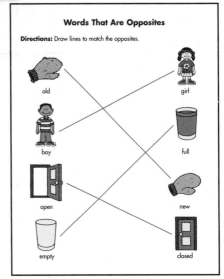

old — new
boy — girl
open — closed
empty — full

214

Words That Are Opposites

Opposites are things that are different. **Up** and **down** are opposites. **Top** and **bottom** are opposites.

Directions: Color and cut out the children. Then, glue the girl **up** at the **top** of the slide. Glue the boy **down** at the **bottom** of the slide.

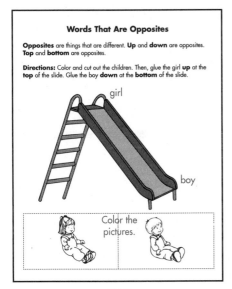

girl

boy

Color the pictures.

215

Words About Friendship

Directions: Use the words in the Word Bank to talk about the picture.

Word Bank				
birthday	party	children	sorry	happy

217

Food Words

Directions: Color the vegetables to help the rabbit find the path to the garden. Use the words in the Word Bank to point to the vegetable each word names.

Word Bank					
tomato	carrot	corn	peas	potato	lettuce

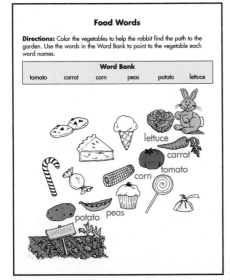

lettuce
carrot
tomato
corn
potato   peas

218

Food Words

Directions: Say the names of each food. Listen to the ending sound. Then, write the ending sound for each word. Color the pictures.

Color the pictures.

brea d
sou p   cor n
frui t   ha m

219

Food Words

Directions: Follow steps 1 through 3 to color the ice-cream cone. Then, trace the words.
1. The top scoop is chocolate.
2. The middle scoop is vanilla.
3. The bottom scoop is strawberry.

ice cream

220

Calendar Words

Directions: Use the calendar to complete each sentence. Circle the correct answer. Then, color your birthday month.

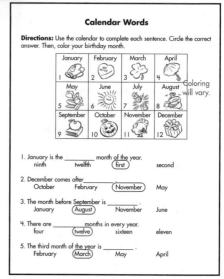

Coloring will vary.

1. January is the _____ month of the year.
   ninth   twelfth   (first)   second

2. December comes after_____
   October   February   (November)   May

3. The month before September is _____.
   January   (August)   November   June

4. There are _____ months in every year.
   four   (twelve)   sixteen   eleven

5. The third month of the year is _____.
   February   (March)   May   April

221

Words That Are Opposites

Directions: Draw lines to match the opposites.

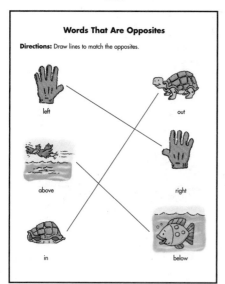

left   out

above   right

in   below

222

Words That Are Opposites

Directions: Color and cut out the birds. Glue one bird **over** the rainbow. Glue the other bird **under** the rainbow. Then, color the rainbow.

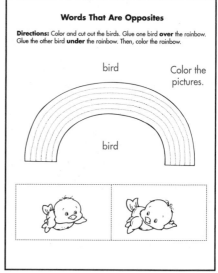

bird

Color the pictures.

bird

223

Words About Friendship

Directions: These two girls are playing hopscotch. Use the words in the Word Bank to talk about the picture.

Word Bank

girls   play   wait   fun   take turns

225

Food Words

Directions: A sandwich and grapes are good for lunch. Color the pictures. Then, answer the questions.

sandwich

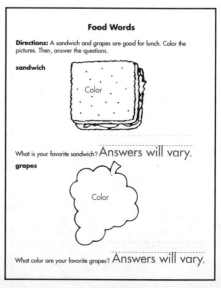

Color

What is your favorite sandwich? Answers will vary.

grapes

Color

What color are your favorite grapes? Answers will vary.

226

Food Words

Directions: Cut out the cards. Put the picture cards in one pile. Put the word cards in another pile. Choose a card from each pile. If the picture matches the word, keep the cards. If not, put them back and try again.

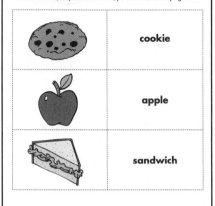

	cookie
	apple
	sandwich

227

Unit 9 Review

Directions: Trace the word in each row. Then, draw a picture to show its opposite.

day	Pictures will vary; each picture should show: night
over	under
sad	happy
small	big
girl	boy

Directions: Think about your favorite month of the year. Tell someone why you like it. Answers will vary.

229

Sequence Words

Directions: First is a sequence word. It tells when something happens. Color the pictures. Then, circle the picture in each row that shows what happened first.

Color the pictures.

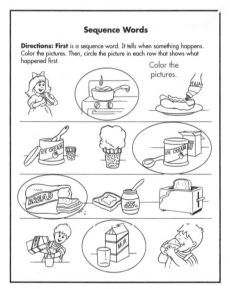

231

Sequence Words

Directions: Next is a sequence word. It tells when something happens. Color the pictures in each row that shows what comes after the first picture. Then, circle the picture.

Color the pictures.

232

Sequence Words

Directions: Last is a sequence word. It tells when something happens. Color the pictures. Then, circle the picture in each row that shows what happened last.

Color the pictures.

233

Words About Living in a City

Directions: Look at the picture. Use the words in the Word Bank to tell what you think it would be like to live in the city. Then, trace and write the word.

Word Bank			
tall	buildings	apartments	crowds
stores	noisy	people	park

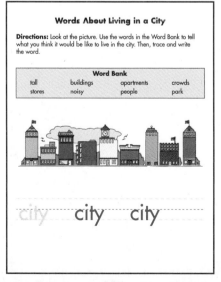

city   city   city

234

Words About the Human Body

Directions: Trace and write the word. Then, answer the question.

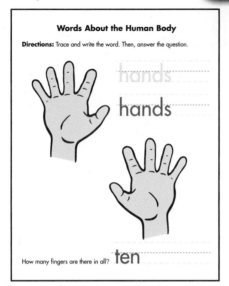

hands

hands

How many fingers are there in all? ten

235

Words About the Human Body

Directions: Trace and write the word. Then, answer the question.

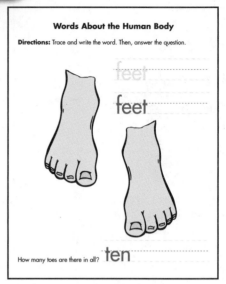

feet

feet

How many toes are there in all? ten

236

Words About the Human Body

Directions: Trace and write the words. Then, color the picture.

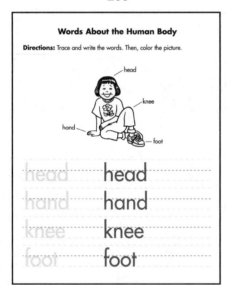

head	head
hand	hand
knee	knee
foot	foot

237

Words About Fractions

Directions: When a shape is divided into two equal parts, each part is called a **half**. Draw the other half of each kite to match. Then, color the kites.

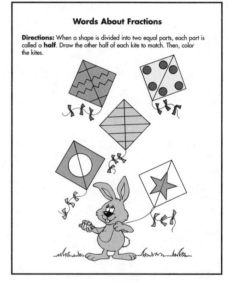

238

Sequence Words

Directions: **Last** is a sequence word. It tells when something happens. Color the pictures. Then, circle the picture in each row that shows what happened last.

Color the pictures.

239

Sequence Words

Directions: **First**, **next**, **then**, and **finally** are sequence words. They tell when something happens. Read the story. Look at the pictures. Then, write the numbers 1, 2, 3, and 4 in the boxes to show the correct order of the story.

First, Ducky packed his things. Next, he went to the airport. Then, he landed. Finally, he was on the island.

240

340

Sequence Words

Directions: After is a sequence word. It tells when something happens. Circle the picture in each row that shows what happened after the first two pictures.

241

Words About Living in the Country

Directions: Look at the picture. Use the words in the Word Bank to tell what you think it would be like to live in the country. Then, trace and write the word.

Word Bank				
plants	trees	hills	road	frog

country   country

242

Words About the Human Body

Directions: Use the words in the Word Bank to complete the picture. Then, color the picture.

Word Bank					
head	neck	arms	hands	legs	feet

Pictures will vary.

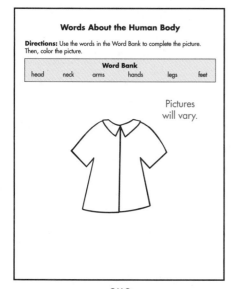

243

Words About the Human Body

Directions: This is Norman. Use the picture to answer the questions about Norman.

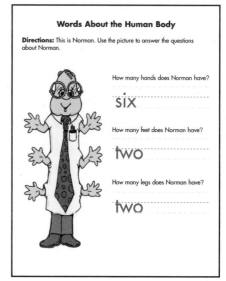

How many hands does Norman have?

six

How many feet does Norman have?

two

How many legs does Norman have?

two

244

Words About the Human Body

Directions: Look at each picture. Which body part is each person using? Draw lines to match the words to the correct pictures.

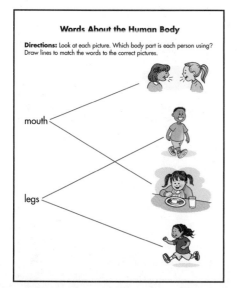

mouth

legs

245

Words About Fractions

Directions: Look at each shape. Color each half a different color. Then, trace and write the word.

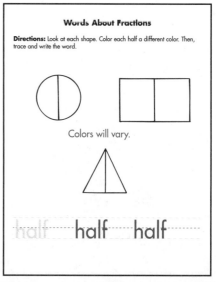

Colors will vary.

half   half   half

246

Sequence Words

Directions: Cut out the pictures. Then, put each set in order to show what happens. Use the words **first**, **next**, and **last** to talk about the pictures.

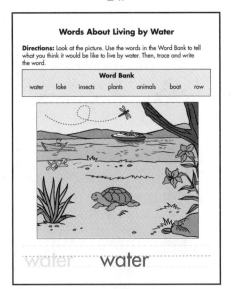

first

first

next

last

next

last

247

Sequence Words

Directions: After is a sequence word. It tells when something happens. Look at the first two pictures. Then, circle the picture that shows what happened after.

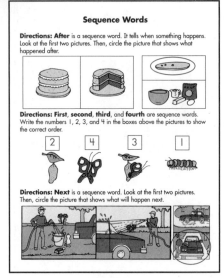

Directions: First, second, third, and **fourth** are sequence words. Write the numbers 1, 2, 3, and 4 in the boxes above the pictures to show the correct order.

2   4   3   1

Directions: Next is a sequence word. Look at the first two pictures. Then, circle the picture that shows what will happen next.

249

Words About Living by Water

Directions: Look at the picture. Use the words in the Word Bank to tell what you think it would be like to live by water. Then, trace and write the word.

Word Bank

water   lake   insects   plants   animals   boat   row

water   water

250

Words About the Human Body

Directions: Trace and write the words.

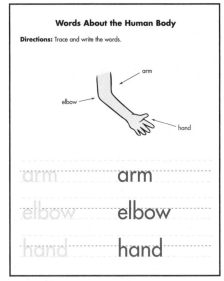

arm

elbow

hand

arm   arm

elbow   elbow

hand   hand

251

Words About the Human Body

Directions: Sing the song. Point to each body part as you sing about it.

Head, shoulders, knees, and toes,
knees and toes.
Head, shoulders, knees, and toes,
knees and toes.
Eyes and ears and mouth and nose.
Head, shoulders, knees, and toes,
knees and toes!

252

Words About the Human Body

Directions: Draw a picture of yourself from head to toe. Label each body part.

Pictures will vary.

253

Unit 10 Review

Directions: Pretend that you are buying a pet. Draw pictures to show what you would do first, next, and last. Talk about your pictures.

Pictures
will vary.

Directions: Draw a picture of the community where you live. Label your picture **city** or **country**.

Pictures will vary.

254

Words in Print

Words are everywhere! They are in books, in newspapers, and even on globes.

Directions: Draw a line from the item on the left to the same item on the right. Then, color the things that are made of paper.

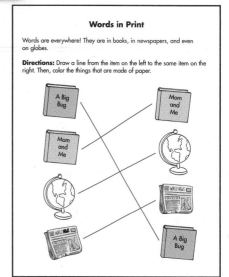

256

Words in Print

Directions: Color the pictures of things you can read. Then, trace and write the word.

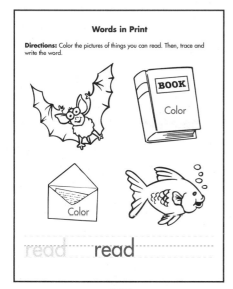

read   read

257

Words in Print

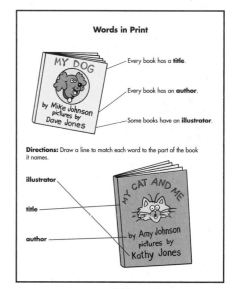

Every book has a **title**.

Every book has an **author**.

Some books have an **illustrator**.

Directions: Draw a line to match each word to the part of the book it names.

illustrator

title

author

258

Celebration Words

Directions: Look at the patterns. At the end of the row, draw the birthday picture that comes next. Then, write the word.

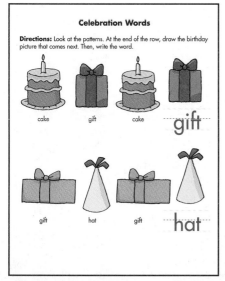

cake   gift   cake   gift

gift   hat   gift   hat

259

Words About Landforms

Directions: A **mountain** is a landform. Connect the dots from 1 to 15. Color the picture. Then, answer the question.

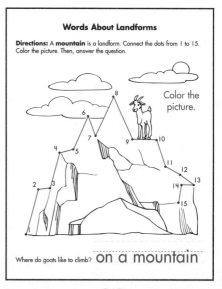

Color the picture.

Where do goats like to climb? on a mountain

260

Words About Landforms

Directions: **Mountains**, **lakes**, **canyons**, and **rivers** are landforms. Draw lines to match the words that are the same. Point to the parts of picture that the words name.

mountain ———— mountain
lake ———— lake
canyon ———— canyon
river ———— river

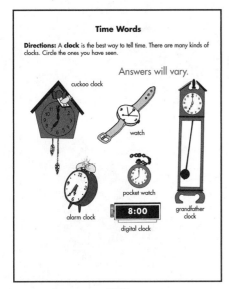

261

Words About Landforms

Directions: **Lakes** and **forests** are landforms. Use the words in the Word Bank to complete the letter. Then, circle the two words in the Word Bank that are landforms.

Word Bank
lake | six
pancakes | forest

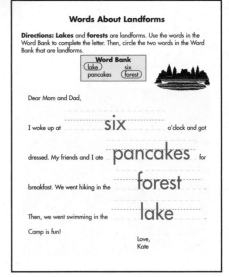

Dear Mom and Dad,

I woke up at **six** o'clock and got

dressed. My friends and I ate **pancakes** for

breakfast. We went hiking in the **forest**.

Then, we went swimming in the **lake**.
Camp is fun!

Love,
Kate

262

Time Words

Directions: A **clock** is the best way to tell time. There are many kinds of clocks. Circle the ones you have seen.

Answers will vary.

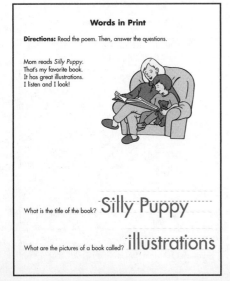

cuckoo clock
watch
pocket watch
alarm clock
8:00
digital clock
grandfather clock

263

Words in Print

Directions: Every story has a title. Read the title of each story. Color the books. Then, trace and write the word.

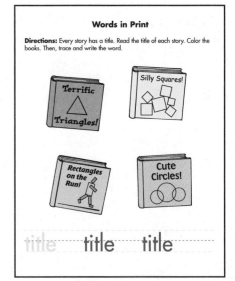

Terrific Triangles!
Silly Squares!
Rectangles on the Run!
Cute Circles!

title   title   title

264

Words in Print

Directions: Read the poem. Then, answer the questions.

Mom reads *Silly Puppy*.
That's my favorite book.
It has great illustrations.
I listen and I look!

What is the title of the book? **Silly Puppy**

What are the pictures of a book called? **illustrations**

265

344

Words About Genre

Directions: A **fairy tale** is a kind of story. *The Gingerbread Man* and *Goldilocks and the Three Bears* are fairy tales. Color the picture from each story. Then, trace and write the words.

Color the pictures.

The Gingerbread Man

Goldilocks and the Three Bears

fairy tale   **fairy tale**

266

Celebration Words

Directions: Circle each picture that shows a birthday word. Then, draw something else you would see at a birthday party.

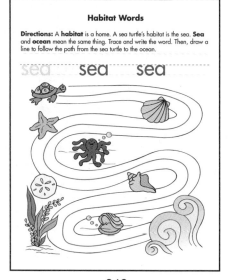

balloons

gift

hat

zipper

Pictures will vary.

267

Words About Landforms

Directions: An **ocean** is a landform. Many animals live in the ocean. Trace and write the word. Then, draw a picture of the ocean and some of the animals that live there.

ocean   ocean

Pictures will vary.

268

Habitat Words

Directions: A **habitat** is a home. A sea turtle's habitat is the sea. **Sea** and **ocean** mean the same thing. Trace and write the word. Then, draw a line to follow the path from the sea turtle to the ocean.

sea   sea   sea

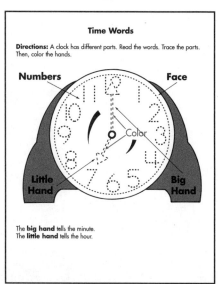

269

Habitat Words

Directions: The swan's habitat is a lake. Trace and write the word. Connect the dots from 1 to 10. Then, color the picture.

lake   lake   lake

Color the picture.

270

Time Words

Directions: A clock has different parts. Read the words. Trace the parts. Then, color the hands.

Numbers   **Face**

Color

Little Hand   **Big Hand**

The **big hand** tells the minute.
The **little hand** tells the hour.

271

Words About Genre

Directions: Read the story about the ant and the lion. Then, answer the question.

Once upon a time, there was an ant and a lion. The lion gave the ant three wishes. The ant's first wish was to ride an elephant. The ant's second wish was to ride an alligator. The ant's last wish was for three more wishes.

Is this story **real** or **fantasy**?   fantasy

272

Words About Genre

Directions: Draw a line to show if each book is real or fantasy.

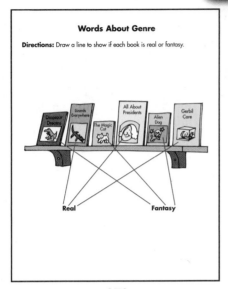

273

Words About Genre

Directions: Fantasy stories are not real. **Real** stories actually happened. Draw an **X** on each thing in the picture that is not real. There are ten.

274

Celebration Words

Directions: A **picnic** is a summertime celebration. Connect the dots from 1 to 10. Color the picture. Then, trace and write the word.

Color the picture.

picnic   picnic

275

Habitat Words

Directions: Draw a line from each animal to its habitat. Then, say the name of the habitat.

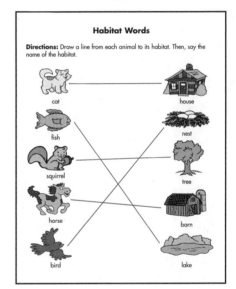

cat — house
fish — nest
squirrel — tree
horse — barn
bird — lake

276

Habitat Words

Directions: Whales and walruses live in the ocean. Trace and write the words.

whale   whale
walrus   walrus
ocean   ocean

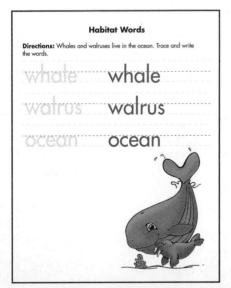

277

Habitat Words

Directions: Circle the animal whose habitat is a cave. Then, write its name on the line.

bat

278

ANSWER key

Unit 11 Review

Directions: Use the words in the Word Bank to write a story about a birthday party. Ask an adult to help you. Be sure to give your story a title.

Word Bank					
hat	gifts	cake	balloons	house	book

Stories will vary.
title

279

Story Words

Directions: Every story has a **character**. A character thinks and talks. A character can even be a talking animal! Draw a line from each character to what it might say.

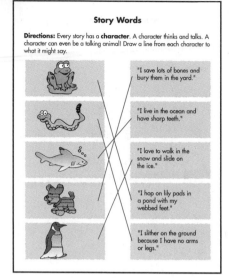

"I save lots of bones and bury them in the yard."

"I live in the ocean and have sharp teeth."

"I love to walk in the snow and slide on the ice."

"I hop on lily pads in a pond with my webbed feet."

"I slither on the ground because I have no arms or legs."

281

Story Words

Directions: A story has a **plot**. The plot is everything that happens in the story. Look at the pictures in each row. Write 1, 2, and 3 in the boxes to show what happened first, second, and third in each story's plot.

282

Story Words

The **setting** tells when and where a story happens.

Directions: Read the story. Then, answer the questions.

It is snowing. My brother and I go outside to play. We build a snowman. Now, it is time for lunch. We go inside. It has been a fun morning!

When does the story happen? winter

Where does the story happen? outside

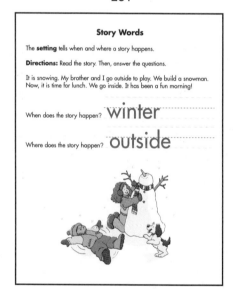

283

Words About the United States

This is the United States of America's flag. It has 50 stars, 7 red stripes, and 6 white stripes.

Directions: Use the words in the Word Bank to describe the American flag.

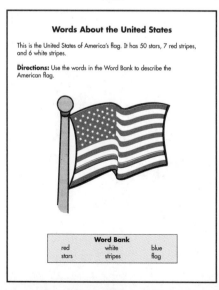

Word Bank		
red	white	blue
stars	stripes	flag

284

347

Words About Water

Directions: Ice is frozen water. Take an ice cube from the freezer. Place it in the sun. Answer the question below.

What does the ice do in the sun? It melts.

285

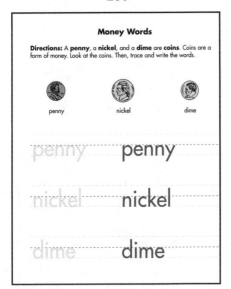

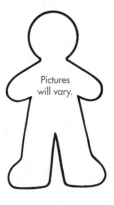

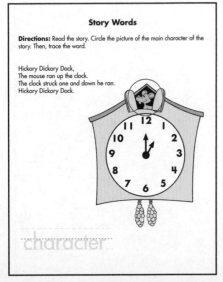

Words About Water

Directions: Water is wet. Trace the word.

wet

286

Words About Water

Water can take different forms. Ice and snow are forms of water. Steam is a form of water, too.

Directions: Circle the picture that answers each question.

Which picture shows water as ice?

Which picture shows water as snow?

Which picture shows water as steam?

287

Money Words

Directions: A **penny**, a **nickel**, and a **dime** are **coins**. Coins are a form of money. Look at the coins. Then, trace and write the words.

penny   nickel   dime

penny   penny

nickel   nickel

dime   dime

288

Story Words

Directions: This is the Gingerbread Man. He is a character in a story. Read the story. Then, complete the picture of the Gingerbread Man.

An old man and his wife lived alone. They had no children. One day, the woman decided to make a gingerbread man. She decorated him with great care. She gave him chocolate chip eyes and a licorice mouth. She gave him three gumdrop buttons. When she was done, the gingerbread man jumped off the table. He ran away singing, "Run, run as fast as you can! You can't catch me. I'm the Gingerbread Man!"

Pictures will vary.

289

Story Words

Directions: Read the story. Circle the picture of the main character of the story. Then, trace the word.

Hickory Dickory Dock,
The mouse ran up the clock.
The clock struck one and down he ran.
Hickory Dickory Dock.

character

290

Story Words

Directions: Use the questions to help tell a story about the picture.

Who is the main character?

What is the setting?

What is the plot?

Stories will vary.

291

Words About the United States

Directions: Here is a map of the United States. Circle the state in which you live. Write the name of your state to complete the sentence.

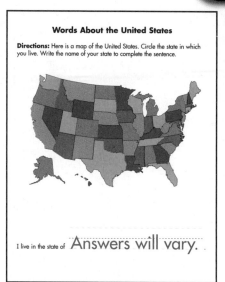

I live in the state of Answers will vary.

292

Words About Water

Directions: These three children are ready to play with water in its different forms. Use the words in the Word Bank to tell two sentences about each child.

Word Bank		
pool	snow	rain
cold	hot	melt

293

Words About Water

Directions: The ice cream will melt if you don't eat it fast! Draw ten sprinkles on the ice cream. Trace the word.

melt

294

Words About Water

Directions: Color the raindrops blue that have water words in them.

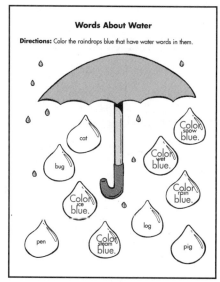

Color snow blue.
Color wet blue.
cat
bug
Color rain blue.
Color ice blue.
log
pen
Color steam blue.
pig

295

Money Words

Directions: Follow the steps 1 through 3 to complete the picture.

1. Color all the **pennies** in the bank brown.
2. Color all the **nickels** in the bank red.
3. Color all the **dimes** in the bank blue.

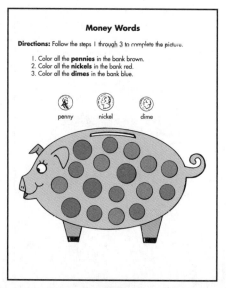

penny   nickel   dime

296

Story Words

Directions: Do you know the story of *Goldilocks and the Three Bears*? This house belongs to the bears. It is the setting of the story. Draw Goldilocks. She is a character in the story. Color the picture. Then, trace the words.

Color the picture.

Picture of Goldilocks will vary.

setting   character

297

Story Words

The **plot** of a story tells what happened.

Directions: Read the sentence. Ask and adult to help you write two sentences that tell what happened next. Then, draw a picture to match the plot of your story.

Sally went to the shelter to choose a new pet.

Sentences will vary.

Pictures will vary.

298

Story Words

Directions: Draw a picture of the main character in your favorite story.

Pictures will vary.

299

Words About the United States

The **president** is the leader of the United States. **George Washington** was the first president. He is called "the father of our country." Here is his picture.

Directions: Color the picture of George Washington.

Color the picture.

300

Words About Water

Directions: Use the words in the Word Bank to write the answers to the riddles. Then, draw the answers.

Word Bank
ocean	watermelon	soap

I am a fruit.
I am red inside.
Water is in my name.
What am I?

watermelon

Pictures will vary.

I am a body of water.
I am salty.
I am home to many fish.
What am I?

ocean

Use me with water.
I make suds.
I help you get clean.
What am I?

soap

301

Words About Water

Think of all the ways you use water at home. You can use water to wash many things, including a dog!

Directions: Circle the word that completes each sentence. Then, write the word on the line.

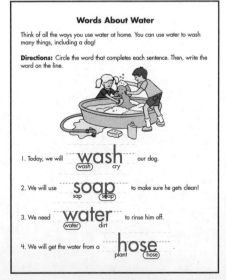

1. Today, we will **wash** our dog.
   (wash) cry

2. We will use **soap** to make sure he gets clean!
   sap (soap)

3. We need **water** to rinse him off.
   (water) dirt

4. We will get the water from a **hose**
   plant (hose)

302

Words About Water

Directions: Water comes in different forms. Look at the picture. The teacup contains hot water. Draw steam coming from the tea. Draw three ice cubes on the table. Draw a puddle on the floor. Then, color the picture.

Color the picture.

303

350

Unit 12 Review

Directions: Draw a line to match each word to its description.

character — the person in a story

ice — frozen water

plot — everything that happens in a story

setting — when and where a story happens

penny — a coin

American flag — something with 50 stars and red and white stripes

304

Notes